The Writer's Guide to Microsoft Word

Kari Holloway

ISBN: 978-1-7337902-9-1
This information was valid at the time of publication and based on the Word 365 2019 edition.
Edited by Brian Paone
Cover designed by Amy Hunter
Formatted by KH Formatting

Contents

Part 1: Microsoft Word

Microsoft Word is the bread and butter for many writers. It is one of the first programs we are introduced to in schools. It comes standard on many computers.

Yet being comfortable with it isn't the same as being familiar with it. I'm comfortable with my car, but that doesn't make me a mechanic.

This guide isn't meant to cover everything possible with Word, but it should make you more aware of the things it can do in a systematic way.

Pilcrow

Pilcrow is an icon on the Home tab in Microsoft Word. It shares space inside the Paragraph subset and next to the Styles section.

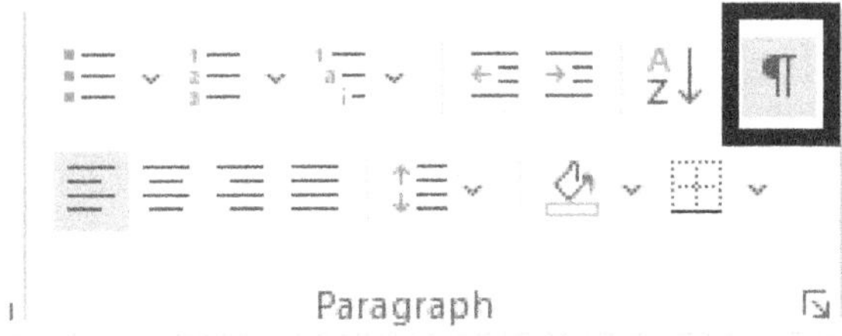

This backward P, sometimes known as the hide-and-show icon, can be annoying when first used, with its strange little symbols, but for formatting, it is your best friend. Those strange little symbols translate to meanings.

To access the symbol guide, click on File > Options.

The Word Options pop-up box will appear in the center of the screen. Click Display > Formatting Marks, and the most common will be listed.

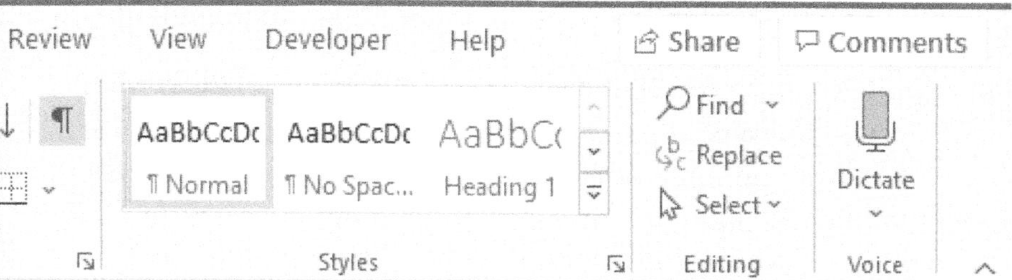

Another way to access the Word Options pop-up box is by right clicking on any of the bars and select Customize the Ribbon.

The symbols that show when Pilcrow is on varies by what you did when typing. For the most part, these are the most common ones.

The ¶ symbol denotes the end of a paragraph. Sometimes the bottom of it has a curve like a lowercase *g*. It takes on traits from the font used.

There are also manual line breaks (created by hold shift + enter), column breaks, page breaks, and a couple of different section breaks.

.... Column Break ....

:::::::::::::: Section Break (Next Page) ::::::::

.... Page Break ....

By understanding the symbols, you can fix these issues when the layout looks wonky.

Font Settings

Located on the Home tab is the Font section. This is where many change the font, make things bigger or smaller, bold, italics, and underline. There are letters beside the size drop-down menu.

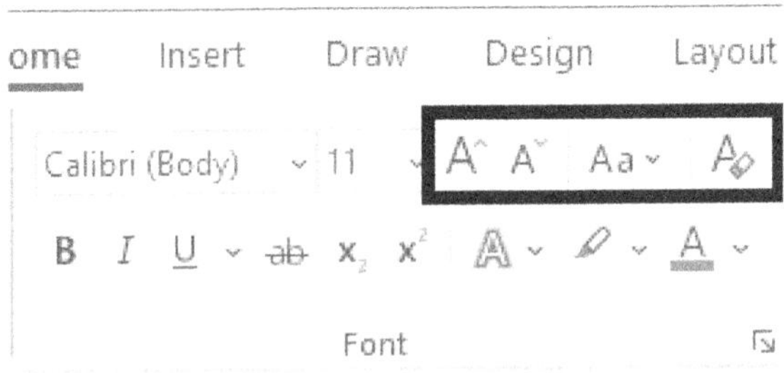

The first A with the arrow pointing up makes the highlighted text larger by 1 size. A in the middle with the arrow pointing down makes highlighted font smaller. This works for different text sizes, enlarging or shrinking all of them. The Aa with the arrow pointing down does five things. The most interesting of these is the lowercase, UPPERCASE, and Capitalize Each Word.

Unlike SMALL CAPS, when the UPPERCASE option is picked, the highlight text will turn to FULL UPPERCASE. If Capitalize Each Word is chosen, The Same Font Will Appear With Each Word Capitalized.

The A with the pink eraser is the last thing to cover in the line of As. Think of this button as a failsafe. This button acts as a undo, erasing all formatting changes and setting it back to "normal" style. Do not confuse it with Ctrl+z or the Undo button located near the Save icon at the top of the page.

Font pop-up box

The Font pop-up box can be accessed via clicking the arrow in the bottom right corner of the Font box or by pressing Ctrl+d.

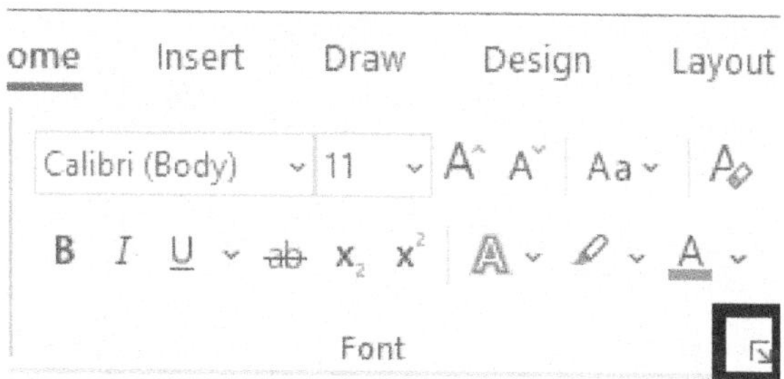

Along with picking font, font style, size, color, and underline, there are some unique features.

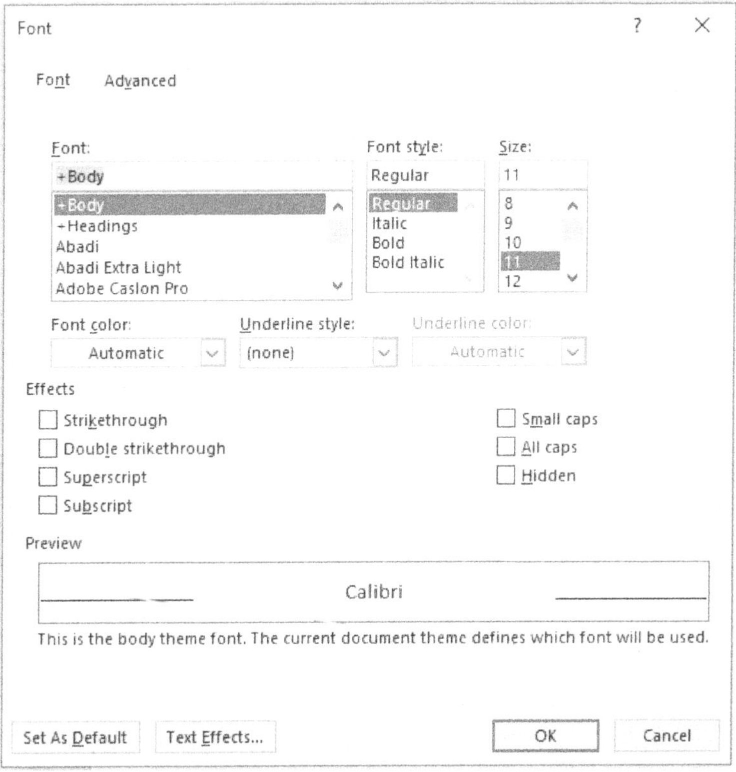

The different effects can be previewed via the preview box. Most are straightforward, but the one I use frequently is SMALL CAPS. Small caps can be used in Headers/Footers or as part of the opening paragraph for chapters for a unique look.

Advanced Options

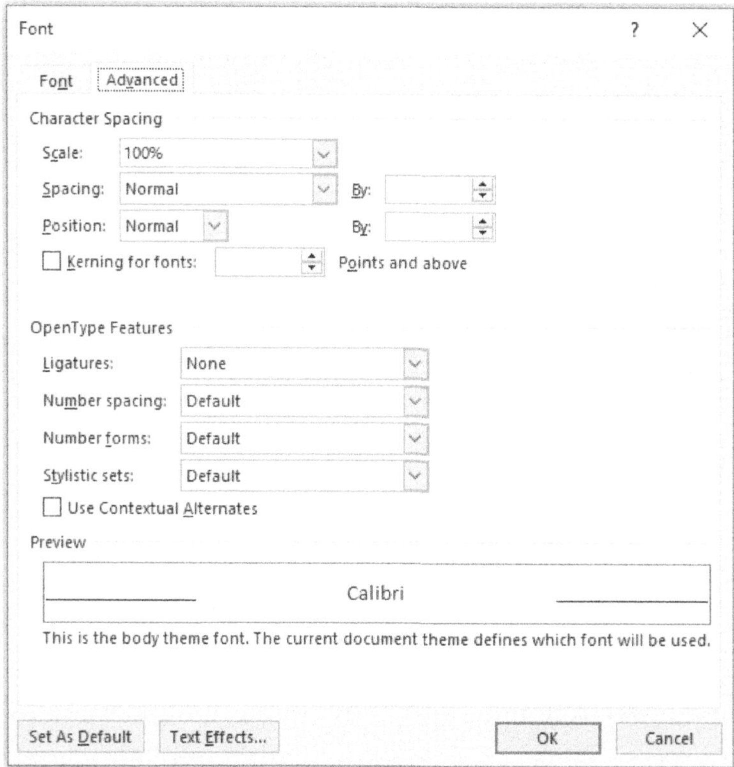

Under Advanced options and then Character Spacing, the spacing between individual characters for entire words are adjusted. Some fonts seem stacked upon each other, and sometimes they seem very far apart. By messing with Spacing (expanded and condensed) by points, the spacing can be more pleasing to the eye and legible.

Example:

The cat ate the rat. (original)

T h e c a t a t e t h e r a t . (character spacing 1.5)

Don't mix Character Spacing with Kerning. Kerning is the space between two characters. Sometimes an italic letter or punctuation invades the space of the next word. Use Kerning to adjust the visual balance and readability between two letters/characters.

Paragraph Settings

The Paragraph box contains the ability to adjust the alignment of the text on the page, the line spacing between lines, indents (not the typical paragraph indent), lists, and the Pilcrow, which we covered earlier.

Most everyone is familiar with the center and left justification. For publication formatting, the fourth option (justified) is used on the prose of the book. This distributes lines of text between the margins, giving it a "clean" look instead of a ragged right-side edge.

Line spacing is the distance between the lines of text. For submission, double space is most common, while for publication, 1.15. It helps with readability, giving readers "white space" to focus on each word.

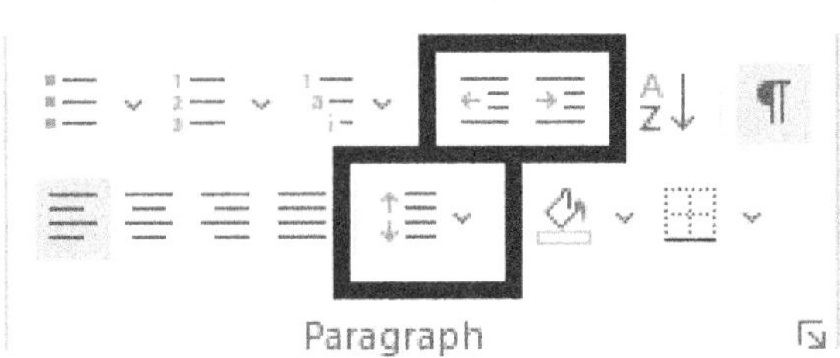

The indent option doesn't indent the first line of the paragraph.

> Instead, this indent option moves the entire paragraph from the margin x-amount of spaces, like how this paragraph is displayed. This can also be accessed via the Layout tab.

Similar to the Font section, the arrow in the bottom right corner of the Paragraph box opens the Paragraph pop-up box.

Paragraph pop-up box

When setting up styles, these options under the Paragraph pop-up box or on the Home bar play roles in adjusting and fine-tuning styles.

Indents & Spacing

Alignment

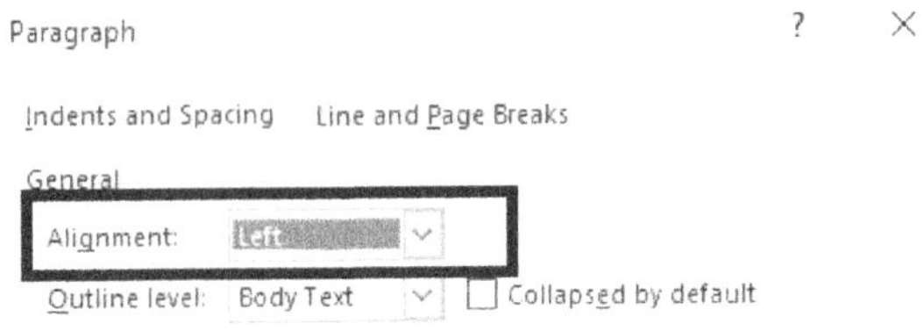

Paragraph ? ×

Indents and Spacing Line and Page Breaks

General

Alignment: Left

Outline level: Body Text Collapsed by default

For chapter titles or scene breaks, they need to be centered. Somethings, like addresses on submissions, need to be left aligned, and the body of the print or eBook texts justified margins are used. If a "manual line break" (shift+enter or a soft return) is used in place of a return/enter, the line of text will be affected and stand out.

It would look similar to this
instead.

When something is centered, check and ensure the text doesn't have indent as well. When people go to center the scene breaks, they don't remove the indent. This causes the scene break, your chapter headings, and even pictures to be an indent off center.

Example:

***

***

It can easily be overlooked in a standard document layout, but it is noticeable in a trade paperback. Autoconverter programs like Draft2Digital and Amazon won't catch this issue.

Indentation

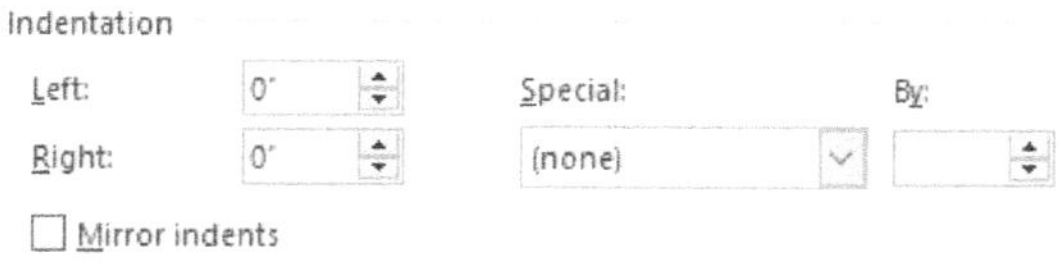

Indentation

Left: 0" Special: By:

Right: 0" (none)

Mirror indents

For fiction submissions, the first line of a paragraph should be indented 0.5" unless otherwise stated. This is also the standard for manuscripts sent to editors. For print publishing, the indent tends to be 0.3" or .25".

To adjust it, leave the Left and Right boxes alone. Under Special, pick "First Line" and enter the indent required.

This paragraph is 0.3".

This paragraph is 0.5".

Correspondents and Quotes

Text messages, handwritten letters, newspaper articles, and epigraphs seem to cause the most confusion for writers.

Text messages are still evolving in a process that is universally accepted, and writer manuals are slow to adapt. To keep it simple, treat it like dialogue, and leave it in italics. It's a form of instant communication.

For handwritten letters, newspapers, and spells recited from tomes, if they are under 3 lines of text (not sentences but lines), leave it in the prose and in italic, like the text message. If the correspondents are over three lines of text, they should be off set in block quotes. If they are in block quote, they can be in italic/script or in regular font. Italic or script can be hard for readers to read, so bump up the size of the font a point or two.

Word has a built-in quote box, but if a new style is created, there are two ways to achieve the block style:

- Paragraph pop-up box—adjust the left and right indentation to .6”.
- Paragraph via Layout tab—adjust the left and right indent to .6”.

An example—

> Torquent nam phasellus. Vehicula quam tincidunt facilisi tellus velit proin vel urna. Ullamcorper natoque ac orci sit sagittis mauris scelerisque eleifend, curae; mollis. Est cubilia est eleifend tristique porttitor leo fames justo hymenaeos. Semper accumsan semper convallis. Tempus, pede sit.

Spacing

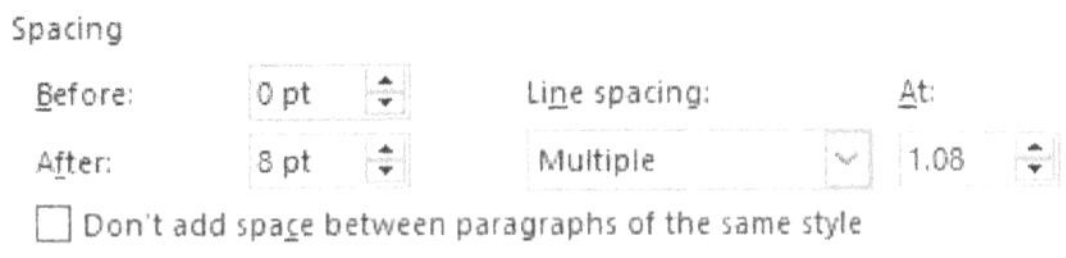

Spacing
Before: 0 pt Line spacing: At:
After: 8 pt Multiple 1.08
☐ Don't add space between paragraphs of the same style

This is where space between paragraphs or styles is set using the Before and After options. This can be used to remove space between similar style paragraphs or add space between paragraphs via the check box option to “Don’t add space between paragraphs of the same style.” Examples would be nonfiction where the paragraphs have spaces between them because the paragraphs are not indented. Another example would be scene breaks, giving the *** or decorative image a little breathing room.

Line spacing is the space between the lines of a paragraph. The most common spacing is single, double, and 1.5 for multiple. Do not use exact or at least. See image for a clear example.

Single	1.15	1.3	1.5
The cat is large and grand. His whiskers were like fishing line, and his eyes like lanterns.	The cat is large and grand. His whiskers were like fishing line, and his eyes like lanterns.	The cat is large and grand. His whiskers were like fishing line, and his eyes like lanterns.	The cat is large and grand. His whiskers were like fishing line, and his eyes like lanterns.

Line and Page Breaks

Paragraph ? X

Indents and Spacing | Line and Page Breaks

Pagination

- [x] Widow/Orphan control
- [ ] Keep with next
- [ ] Keep lines together
- [ ] Page break before

Formatting exceptions

- [ ] Suppress line numbers
- [ ] Don't hyphenate

Textbox options

Tight wrap:

None

Preview

Sample Text Sample Text Sample Text Sample Text Sample Text Sample Text Sample Text Sample Text
Sample Text Sample Text Sample Text Sample Text Sample Text Sample Text Sample Text Sample Text
Sample Text Sample Text Sample Text Sample Text Sample Text

Tabs... Set As Default OK Cancel

Widow/Orphan control

Window/Orphan controls is a misunderstood aspect.

When only the last line of the paragraph appears at the top of the next page, that line is called a *widow*. When only the first line of the paragraph appears at the bottom of the first page, that line is called an *orphan*. I'm assuming they are called widow and orphan because the line is "abandoned" from its "family" paragraph. Keep it checked to reduce the dangling one-liners from looking lost.

Keep with next

Keep with next takes different styles or different paragraphs and links them into one item, so they don't break across different pages. Highlight what needs to be kept together as one thing, and use Keep with next option.

Keep lines together

Keep lines together is similar to Keep with next. This keeps an entire paragraph together instead of letting it break across multiple pages.

Paragraph Starters

For fiction, there are multiple ways to start the first paragraph of a chapter or after a scene break.

This is a standard paragraph starter. It is not indented and is flush with margin. It's how most books begin.

THIS IS A MICROCAP option. The first 4 to 5 words are highlighted and using the Font pop-up box.

This is a drop cap. To apply, pick Drop Cap on the Insert tab. There are two styles of drop cap, but the "Dropped" one is more common.

There is one issue to note with drop caps. Even though the height of the drop cap can be adjusted, 3 lines is standard, and sometimes the starter paragraph doesn't contain as many lines needed to keep the next paragraph from occupying the bottom of the drop cap.

Example of a drop cap issue.

See this odd space. This is what happens when the starter paragraph does not cover the number of lines needed to occupy the drop cap.

In these cases, just remove the indent from the paragraph to keep it flush to hold to an aesthetically pleasing look. Do not adjust the height of the drop cap unless you plan to redo all of them.

Styles

We've covered Font and Paragraph areas, and now we move along the Home tab to the Styles section. To many, these are foreign letters with little meaning aside from making things bigger and turning things blue.

Styles are like a prepackaged meal. They are time savers and can be copied between documents, crafted to suit your needs, and easy to adjust.

`Most Microsoft documents start with normal styles, like this paragraph. This is the style that everyone is familiar with.`

At the base of the Styles section is the little arrow that expands into the Styles Panel.

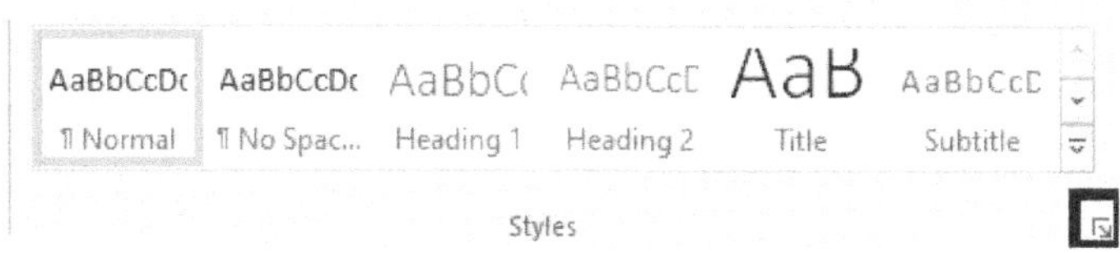

Unlike Font and Paragraph pop-up boxes, Styles Panel is a vertical column. All the styles in the document are displayed.

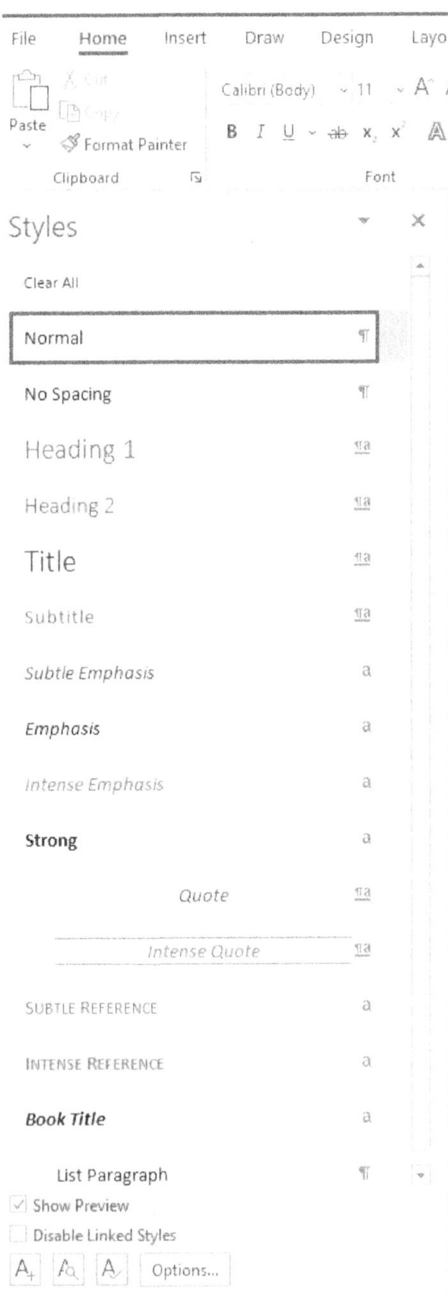
File
Home
Insert
Draw
Design
Layou
Paste
Format Painter
Clipboard
Calibri (Body)
11
Font
Styles
Clear All
Normal
No Spacing
Heading 1
Heading 2
Title
Subtitle
Subtle Emphasis
Emphasis
Intense Emphasis
Strong
Quote
Intense Quote
SUBTLE REFERENCE
INTENSE REFERENCE
Book Title
List Paragraph
Show Preview
Disable Linked Styles
Options...

Now to cover some of the preexisting ones. Heading (1-6) helps create the table of contents and enable navigation within the document.

There are other presets—links, normal, Title, header (not to be confused with Heading) and footer—built into every new document, and their layout is automatic. They can be modified.

Looking at the options at the bottom of the Styles panel, there are options: create, inspect, managed, and options.

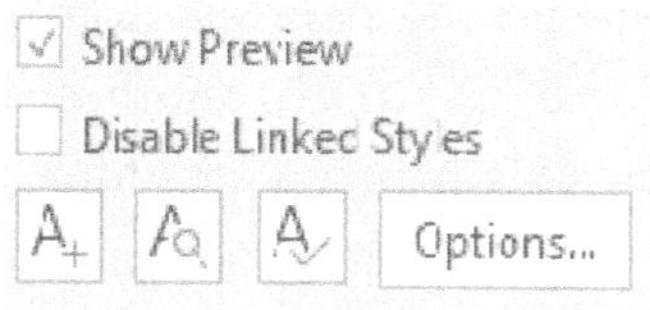

A+ —creating a style

When a paragraph is laid out the way it needs to be, leave the cursor inside that paragraph, and click the A+ to create a new style, and the Create New Style From Formatting pop-up box will appear.

Give it a name that you can associate with that layout. Having paragraph 1, 2, 3, etc. won't save you time a year from now when you need that specific style again. You can modify the name as often as need be.

Modifying Styles

If a font needs changes in style name, font, font size, spacing, indents, or any other finer details of a paragraph style, there are two ways:

- By adjusting the paragraph in the document and having the style Update to match via either the Styles portion of the Home Bar OR by clicking the dropdown menu next to the style in the Styles Panel.
- By clicking Modify (located in the same spot as Update to Match) and adjusting in the Style pop-up box. The Format dropdown menu gives access to Paragraph and Font settings covered earlier.

When a style is modified, the update takes effect through the entire document. Example: Submission guidelines want Courier, but the file is in Times New Roman. Open the style, change the font, and hit Apply. Another example would be in publishing, when a Chapter Title's font or size is changed. This saves time by not having to manually find every Chapter 1, 2, 3 and change them.

Under Modify, there is the Automatically Update option. Leave it unclicked. When it is clicked, any adjustment made to a paragraph that a style is applied to will automatically be applied to all the styles. IE: A bullet point is used on a normal style, now all the normal styles now have bullet points.

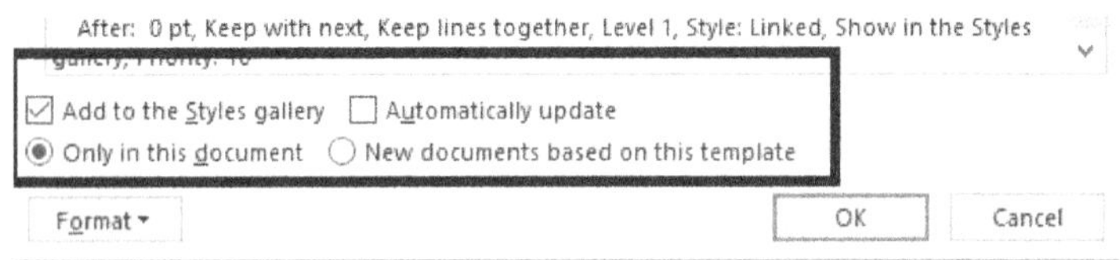

Import/Export Styles

Styles can be imported between documents. This can save time between submissions or publications, since the styles do not have to be recreated.

This is achieved through the Developer Option. To add it to Word:

Click File > Options > Customize Ribbon.

Change the drop-down menu under Choose Commands to Main tabs and click on Developer. Add it to the right-side menu. Click Okay.

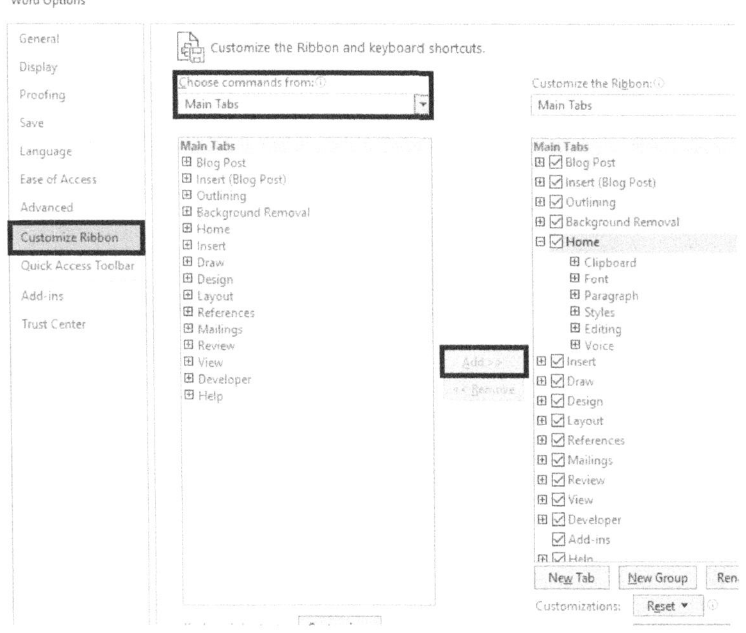

Back inside the document, click on the Developer tab and choose Document Template.

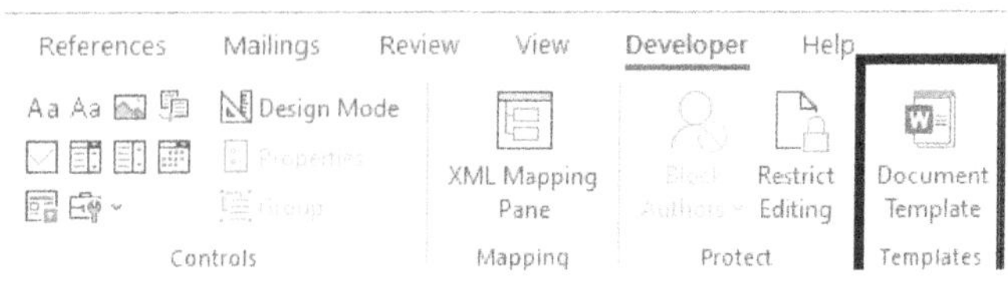

The Templates and Add-ins pop-up box will open.

Ignoring everything else, click on Organizer in the bottom corner. This opens the Organizer where styles can be import or export from one document to another document.

The document receiving the styles should be on the left side, and the document the styles are being copied from on the right side. To change either, click Close File on the Organizer pop-up and Open File.

Word automatically defaults to looking for a template. Change the option from Templates to All Word Documents or All Files. Pick the style importing file and click Open.

Labeled styles are easier to import. It's the difference between importing paragraph 1, 2, 3 when only Scene Break Lighting Bolt is needed.

Click the style and hit Copy. The style will appear in the left-hand column. To import multiple styles, hold Ctrl. Once finished, click Close.

Layout

The Layout tab holds familiar parts (Paragraph) and the ability to adjust Size, Margins, and insert Breaks.

Margins and Sizes can be accessed via the arrow in the corner of the section or drop-down menu beneath each word.

Margins control the "white space" around the edge of the paper. Orientation is landscape or portrait. Size affects how big or small the page is. Columns are how many rows of text there are on a page.

If the section is accessed via the bottom corner, there are three options: Margins, Paper, Layout. Writers only need to be concerned with Margins and Paper.

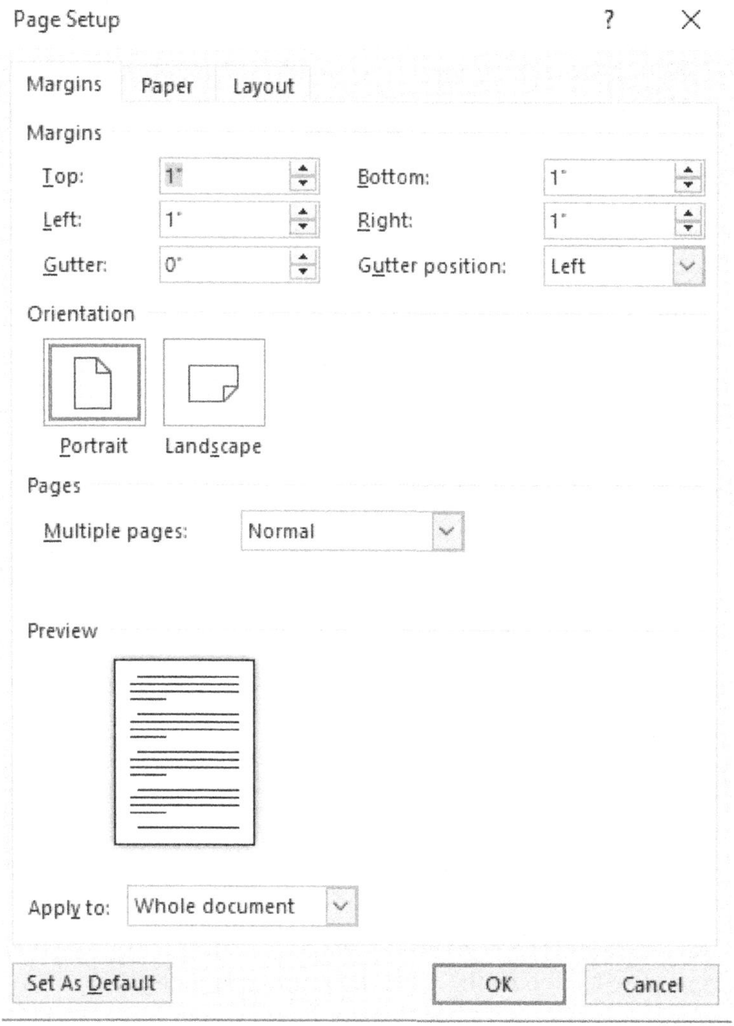

Page Setup ? ×

Margins | Paper | Layout

Margins

Top: 1" Bottom: 1"

Left: 1" Right: 1"

Gutter: 0" Gutter position: Left

Orientation

Portrait Landscape

Pages

Multiple pages: Normal

Preview

Apply to: Whole document

Set As Default OK Cancel

Margins

Margins give people a place to hold or staple/bind without compromising the printed work. The default setting in Word are 1" margins on all four sides. If a book contained the same margins, there would be few words on the page. Books are printed with mirror margins. To access that option, click Margins > Pages > Multiple Pages drop-down menu > Mirror Margins. A good basic starting margin for books are .6 top, bottom, and outside margin. Inner margins .75 or .8 if the gutter is set to zero.

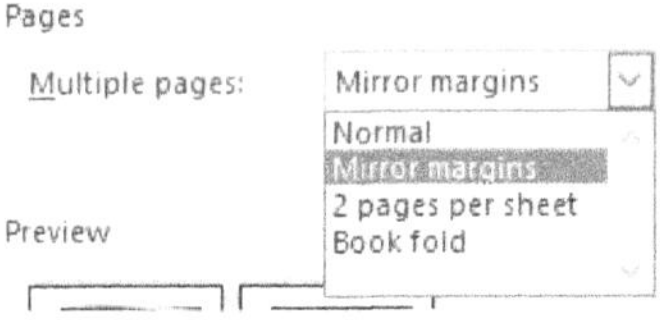

Depending on the POD used, they will have guidelines on how small margins can be.

Gutter

The gutter is the distance between the inside margins. For a .8" inner margin, the gutter would be 1.6". Many formatters tack the distance on the inside margins and leave the gutter at zero instead of messing with the gutter numbers.

Here's how the gutter works. If the inside margin needs to be 0.75", the inside margin + the gutter would need to equal .75". 0.13" & 0.62", or 0.32" & 0.43" … or any combination of numbers that total 0.75". That's a lot of math. There are threads on K-boards and other forums talking about gutters for more information.

To Bleed or Not to Bleed

What is bleed?

Bleed is described as a "document which has images or elements that touch the edge of the page, extending beyond the trim edge and leaving no white margin." Convoluted? Maybe. A good example would be children's illustrated books where the images stretch from the edge of the page to the other edge.

To see if a file has bleed, check the page size in the PDF. If the pages are slightly larger than the trim, then the file has bleed. If the pages are exact, then the file does not have bleed.

The standard bleed is .125" to top, .125" to outside, and .125" to bottom. A 6" by 9" becomes a 6.125" by 9.25." Different PODs have different guidelines, so double check with them prior to formatting.

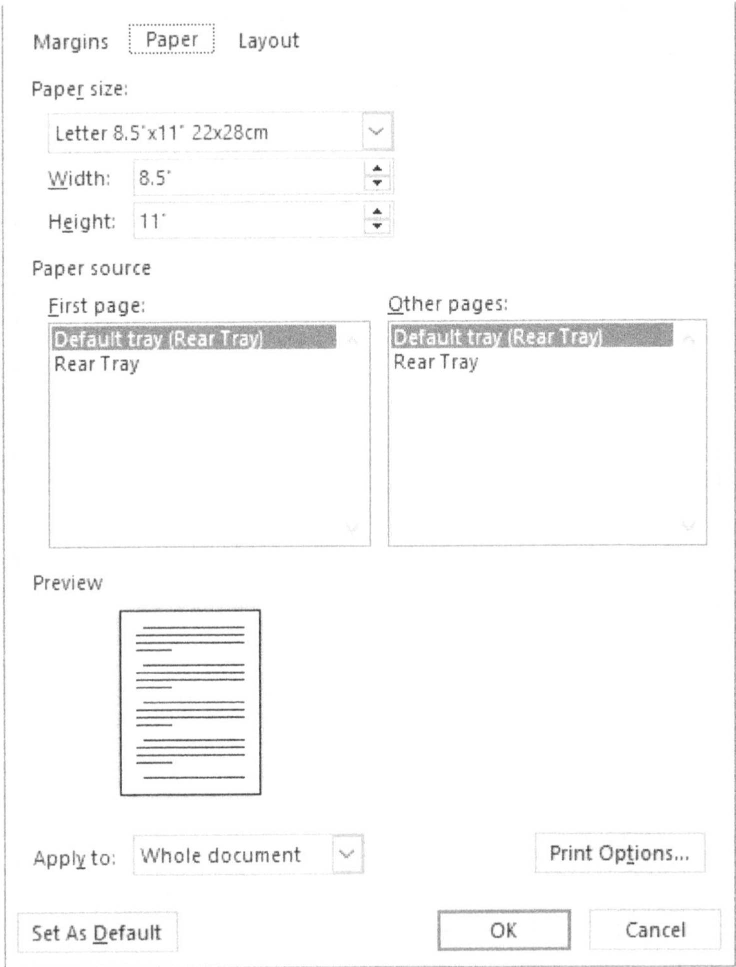

Sizes

Sizes refer to paper sizes and determine what size/trim the pages are. The default setting is for standard printer paper, 8.5" by 11". By adjusting the width and height and applying it to the whole document, the trim size can be set.

Page Breaks vs Section Breaks

Page Breaks and Section Breaks serve similar yet different purposes. If the Pilcrow is on, the breaks will be clearly labeled Page Break and Section Breaks.

Page Breaks

Page Breaks help separate content and is an option for starting something on the next page instead of using multiple enter/ returns. This can be found in three spots:

- Layout tab > Breaks
- Insert tab > Page Breaks
- Pressing Ctrl+Enter

If a font has been changed or a trim size adjusted and the chapter did not stay at the beginning of a new page, it is because a page break was not used to move the start of the chapter to the next page.

eBook converters use Page Breaks to determine where new chapters are, and in print layout, inserting a page break to move things around adjust the layouts without adjusting the header/footer.

Section Breaks

A section break is not a scene break. It creates different sections. For writers this would be front matter, chapters, and back matter. A section break causes the header/footer to "start" over.

There are four section break options under Breaks on the Layout tab, and the information provided by Word explains them.

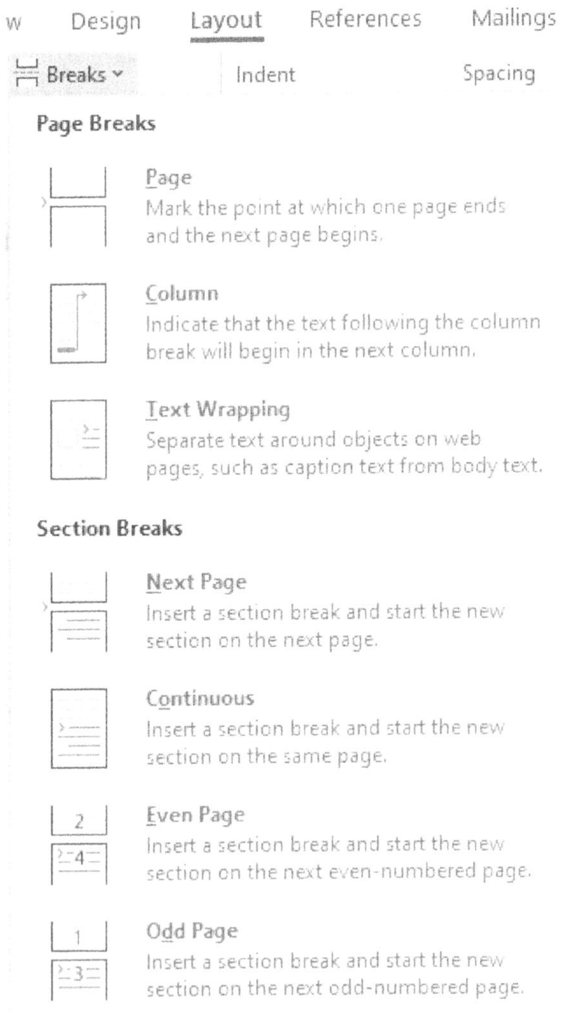

w Design Layout References Mailings

Breaks Indent Spacing

Page Breaks

Page
Mark the point at which one page ends and the next page begins.

Column
Indicate that the text following the column break will begin in the next column.

Text Wrapping
Separate text around objects on web pages, such as caption text from body text.

Section Breaks

Next Page
Insert a section break and start the new section on the next page.

Continuous
Insert a section break and start the new section on the same page.

Even Page
Insert a section break and start the new section on the next even-numbered page.

Odd Page
Insert a section break and start the new section on the next odd-numbered page.

Headers and Footers

To access the Headers and Footers, double click in the top or bottom margin of a page.

For the Header, double click on the top of the page. Names, Titles, and Submission information is applied to headers.

To go to the footer, double click in the bottom of the page, or click "Go to Footer" on the special tab that opens when the header/footer is engaged. The footer generally contains page numbers.

Word comes with built-in layout options for the header/ footer via the drop-down menu for each, and coupled with design options (below), paragraph and font settings, unique ones can be crafted.

There are three options when it comes to designing.

- The header/footer can be the same. Uncheck the "Different First Page" and "Different Odd & Even Pages."
- The header/footer can be different depending on if the page is even and odd. Click "Different Odd & Even Pages."
- The header/footer on the first page of a section can be different from the header/footer that precedes it until it hits a section break. Click "Different First Page."

By applying the options, the header/footer for submissions and for books can be produced.

To change the header/footer, such as in a collection where the story titles are different, the header/footer needs to be "unlinked" from the previous section.

Apply the section break > click Link to Previous to uncouple the current page section from the previous > Adjust that header. Depending on the layout, the header/footer for that section will need to be unlinked before adjusting the header/footer on that page. Example: unlinking the even page and trying to adjust the odd page. To fix that, the odd page must be unlinked as well if the "Different Odd & Even Page" option is chosen.

If the headers aren't flowing correctly between sections, make sure the header/footer design options match the first section.

Unique headers/footers can be designed using the paragraph and font settings and saved as a style.

Writer Trick #1

If you do not like the space the header and footer take up while writing, you can hide them. Hover the mouse between the two pages, wait for the icon to appear and click.

Page Numbers

Page number locations are subjective. Sometimes they are in the footer, and other times they are in the header. When the page number option is clicked, a drop-down menu appears with various options. These options, the paragraph alignment and "Current Position," can shift the page number location in the Header/Footer Bar.

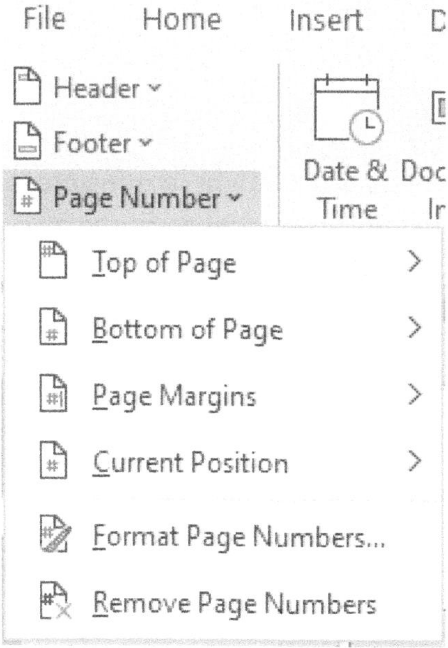

Format Page Numbers opens the Page Number Format pop-up box. The Number format drop-down menu offers roman numerals to standard numbers. Page numbering lets the page numbers flow from a previous section (i.e. the last page was page 13, and after a section break, the next page is 14), or the page number can be chosen for that particular section (i.e. after a section break, Chapter 1 starts on page 1).

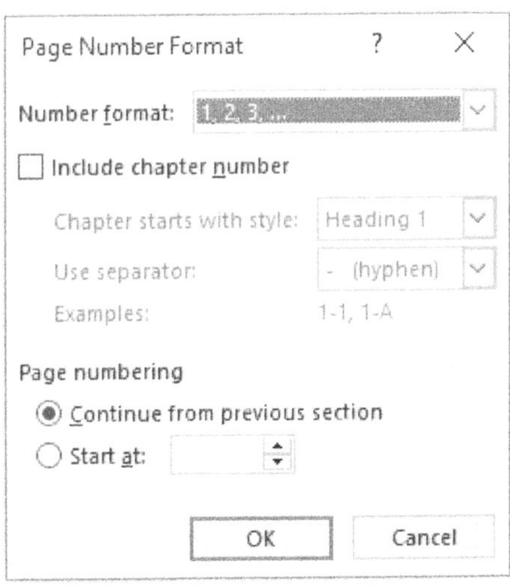

If the margins do not look right in mirror margins, go to the first page of the document and see if the page number is set to 0 or 1. It should be set to page 1, and this works even if the page number is not visible.

Table of Contents

If Headings (1-6) are used in the document, Word can generate a table of Contents (TOC). This option can be found on the Reference tab. The first option is Table of Contents, and Word has a few built-in options, but generally, clicking "Custom table of Contents" works well.

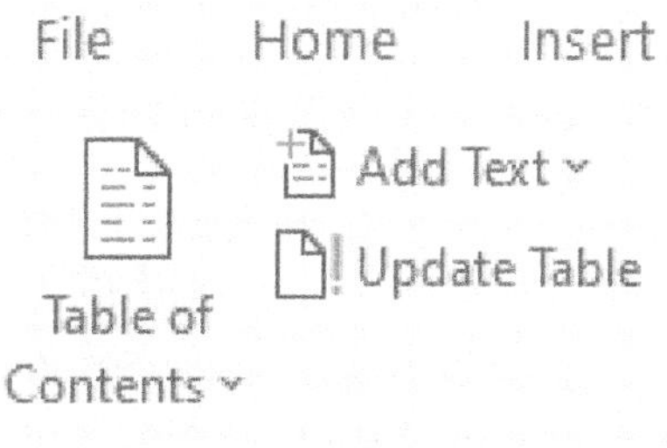

The generated TOC will auto adjust page numbers if the "show page numbers" option is used. Similar to adjusting the header/footer and styles, the font, font size, and spacing can be modified.

Navigation Panel

The neat feature about Headings is the same outline that would be generated in the table of contents can appear under Navigation Panel. There are two ways of finding the panel.

- Click Find / Ctrl+F
- View > Navigation Pane

The Navigation Panel appears on the left-hand side and has three options:

- Headings
- Pages
- Results.

Headings

Things that have Heading (1-6) style will appear here, and it resembles how the table of contents will look when generated.

By using the panel, you can navigate to different sections quickly instead of scrolling, and information nestled under a Heading can be dragged/dropped without copy and pasting it. To move things around, hover the mouse over the wording, click and hold and drag to the new location.

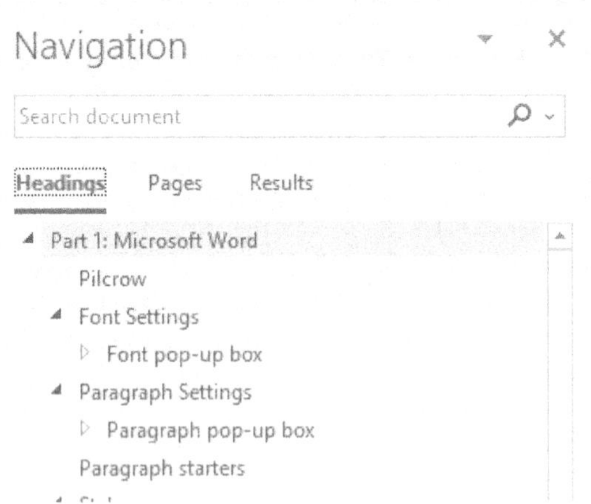

Pages

If nothing is being searched, Pages shows all the pages. If the search feature is being used, then the pages containing the search phrase will be displayed. Those pages will have the search phrase highlighted in yellow and the page number beneath it.

Results

Results is a zoomed in result for the search phrase. Instead of seeing a list of pages and numbers, the word/phrase around the search terms are shown.

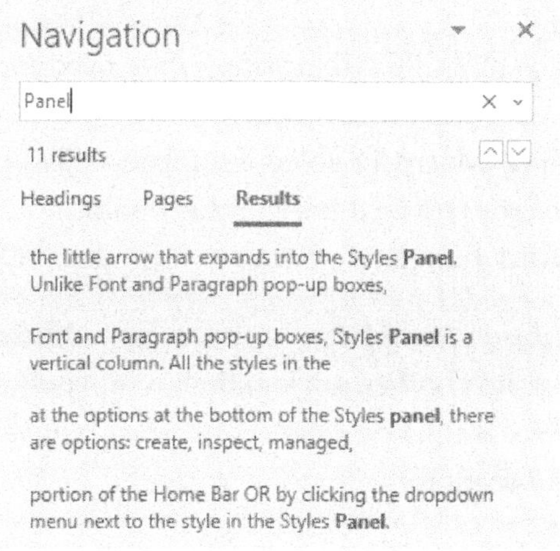

Templates

The groundwork for templates has been laid. Templates are Word documents that come with preprogramed styles and information.

The most common document is Blank Document. It's the default blank document most people use.

To make a new template, open a new Word document. Set the areas needed: margins, styles, even information such as name, address, header/footer information.

Once the layout is done, click Save As. There are three options:

- Word 97-2003 Template—Files needing to be saved in .doc instead of .docx.
- Word Macro-Enabled Template—Files that contain macros (covered later in this book).
- Word Template—Files saved in .docx. Use this one.

To find created templates, open a new Microsoft Word document. Click on Personal, and all templates made should be listed here. If it's a popular template, it will also appear in the Featured section.

To modify the template, open the template, modify it and save the new template as a different file name or override the previous template.

Links and Bookmarks

Link is one way to embed a hyperlink. If the need arises for all hyperlinks to be broken/removed, highlight the links (or Ctrl+A to select the entire document) and press Ctrl+Shift+F9. Make sure the link contains the http:// and is not linking to the computer desktop.

Located beside Link is Bookmarks, and they can be used in place of Heading (1-6). This comes in handy at times when images are used for chapter titles or media packets are created in Word.

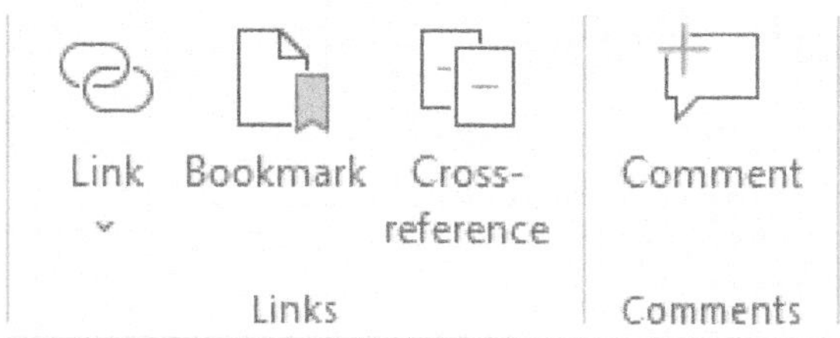

Put the cursor where a "link" needs to be. Click Bookmark. Name the point exactly how it needs to appear in the table of contents.

Find and Replace

Find and Replace isn't just for spelling errors and name changes. Under the various options that the Find and Replace pop-up box gives under the "more" option, a document can be combed for particular styles, words in certain font/size, highlighted, and more.

Format leads to a variety of options:

- Font (type, size, bold, italic)
- Paragraph settings (the exact pop-up box covered earlier)
- Styles
- Highlight and more

Special leads to some unique items.

- Line breaks
- Dashes
- Caret Characters
- Nonbreaking Spaces and more

Here is a quick list of commonly searched things. To remove them in a document, find them and replace with nothing.

^p = paragraph marks

- This is how Word determines where a paragraph ends.
- To remove spaces at the end of a paragraph, search for [space ^p] and replace with [^p]. (replace the word space with an actual space)
- To remove spaces at the beginning of a paragraph, search for [^p space] and replace with [^p].

^t = tab

- There should be no tabs in a document. Indents should be set by the Paragraph settings.

^s = nonbreaking space

- A nonbreaking space is a space that will not let a word hyphen. It might be used around a name like J.K. Rowling to keep her name from splitting between two lines.

^m = Page Breaks

^b = Section Breaks

^l (lower case L) = manual line break

- A manual line break is created by pressing Shift+Enter
- If these are in the document, replace with a paragraph mark [^p] to keep Word from turning multiple paragraphs into a single paragraph

The Review tab

The Review tab is a writer's best friend. It contains:

Proofing—the built-in spell and grammar checker that gives the red and blue squiggle lines.

Readaloud—a built-in readaloud system that will read the document. It isn't the best feature, but it does a decent job

Track changes—Used mainly by editors or beta readers, this allows changes to be "transposed" over the document without making concrete changes until accepted.

Compare features—allows two documents to be compared against each other and the differences highlighted in a system similar to Track Changes.

Track Changes

Track Changes has three parts:

- Comments
- Tracking
- Changes

Comments are messages left for specific areas. They can be used without turning Track Changes on or off. Place the cursor or highlight the words, click New Comment, and a chat bubble will appear. They can be removed via the Delete option next to New Comment. Comments can be scrolled through with the Previous and Next in the same section.

To turn Track Changes on or off, click the Track Changes icon on the tracking bar or chose the first option via the drop-down menu. The second option under that menu prevents track changes from being used.

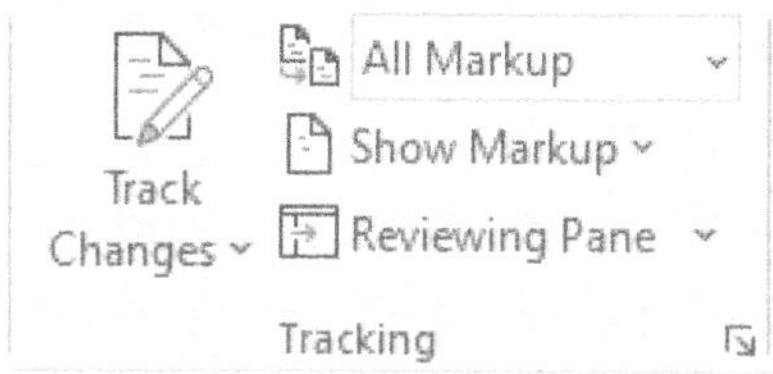

While track changes is active, all changes, comments, and such are "imposed" on top of the document and appear in different colors, underlined, and sometimes highlighted if a comment has been made.

To see all the changes, the drop-down menu beside Track Changes should be on All Markup. Show Markup lets the writer sort through which type of tracking they want to see. The Reviewing Pane gives a panel similar to the Navigation and Style panel where all the changes are shown.

Accept or reject the changes to add the changes to the document or remove the change suggestion. To flip between the changes, use the Previous and Next buttons beside the Accept and Reject.

Unresolved track changes and comments can sometimes appear in PDFs and eBooks.

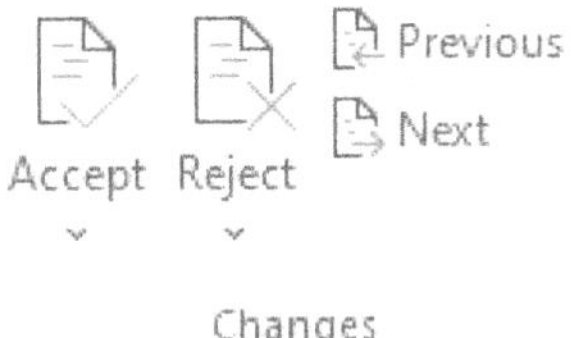

Compare

Compare takes two files and compares them, making the differences between the documents noticeable in track changes. There are two options:

- Compare a document side by side
- Combine two documents into one

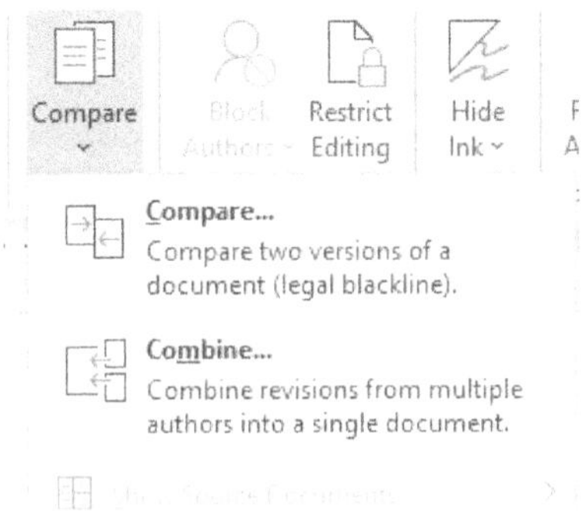

Combining two documents into one can be useful when receiving files from beta readers. The same document has been returned with comments and suggestions from various people. To help this make sense, the new documents are B,

C, D, and E. The original file is A. Changes made to B might make changes to D irrelevant, or that great idea in C for a paragraph might be lost to memory while tackling with trying to make changes to B, D, E and updating A. Instead, using combine B and C becomes F, D and E become G, F and G become H, and A joins H to become the new document of A where all the changes can be worked through in a single document with all the comments and track changes.

Comparing two documents can be useful if there are documents that look the same but are unsure if any changes have been made. Word will create a document that shows differences in Track Changes, and that document can be saved as a new file. Do not confuse the Compare function to the Combine function.

Experiment with smaller examples, like a short story that spans only a few pages, before attempting to do this with novels as it can become confusing on larger scales.

Combine Feature

Projects may have different parts. An anthology has multiple authors, and with that comes multiple files, and a book could be saved by the chapter instead of one long document. Instead of opening each file, copy and pasting into a single file saves time by using the Combine Feature on the Insert tab.

To combine two files into one, open the first document and scroll to where the next document/section needs to be added. Click on the Insert tab, and located near the Drop Cap option is the drop-down menu Object. Choose Text from File.

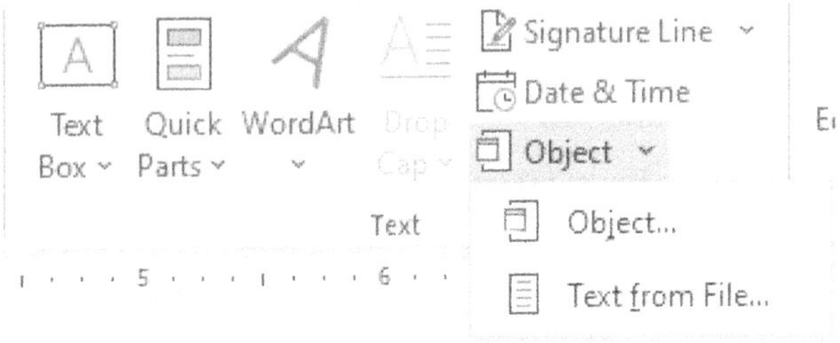

The styles associated with the importing document will transfer along with the exact file layout that is being imported.

Try this option with a template, and double check your work. Any mistakes in the original files will transfer in with the text.

Footnotes, Endnotes, and Citations

Before explaining how to craft these, let's cover what footnotes, endnotes, and citations are.

Notes and citations are used mainly in peer-review journals or works of nonfiction, and they play a role in providing references for ideas or items used to support or disprove the book's premise.

Depending on the type of writing, how notes and citations are used is covered by the writer's manual (APA, MLA, CMoS), and this places the referenced material in one of three locations and places the reference material in one of three locations.

> Citation—happens within the text and are offset by parentheses. They include the author, the title, and the date of publication, along with specific page numbers. Most commonly found within research papers.
>
> Footnotes—generated in the footer of the page. They are similar to citations but may contain a short explanation.
>
> Endnotes—generated at the end of the chapter or at the end of the book. These notes can be longer and more detailed.

Footnotes and Endnotes are the most common in the book world. Both provide writers with a clear method of directing readers to further information on the subject. The terms are used interchangeably, but the location and function determine which one is appropriate to use.

To create an endnote or footnote, click on the References tab. Highlight or set the cursor where the note needs to be placed, and click Insert Footnote or Endnote. When one is applied, a number will appear in the document, and a corresponding one will appear in the footer or at the end of the chapter/ document.

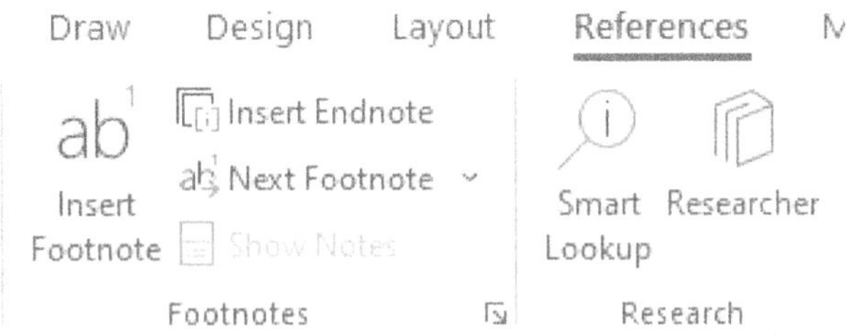

To cycle through the footnotes, click the Next Footnote, or choose the correct drop-down menu option to choose next/ previous footnotes/endnotes.

To remove a footnote/endnote, delete the reference number in the body of text. The footnote will be removed, and the notes that come after will update the numbers accordingly.

Endnotes/footnotes can be useful in drafts for writers to leave notes with keywords to research later. This is better in some instances than leaving a comment, because footnotes are printable.

In eBooks, footnotes should be changed to endnotes, and Word can do that. To do this, click on the bottom arrow of the Footnotes box. The Footnotes and Endnotes pop-up box will appear. Under the Location section, click Convert.

- The first option converts all footnotes to endnotes.
- The second option converts all endnotes to footnotes.
- The third option swaps all footnotes and endnotes in the case that both are within a document.

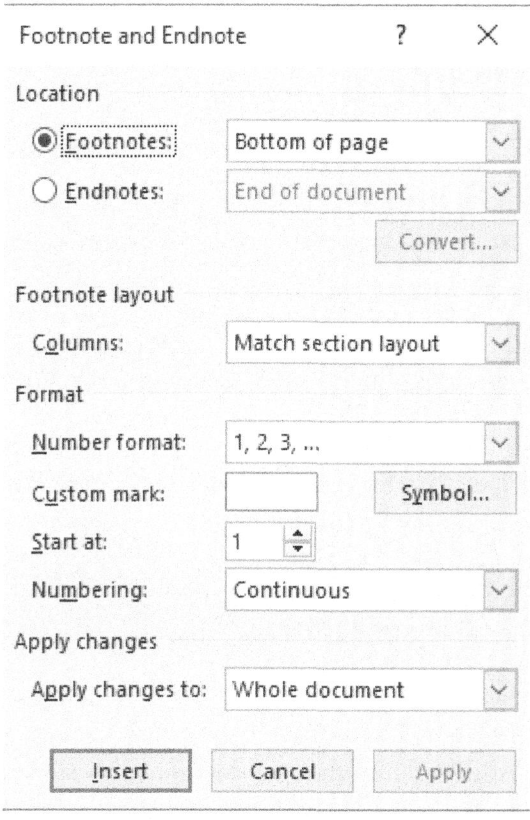

Citations

Word has a built-in ability to save and produce citations. These can be useful for reference guides or college papers but not for novels. On the Citations and Bibliography section, the drop-down style menu gives the most common layouts for APA, MLA, etc.

To add citations, click Insert Citation. Two options will appear:

Add New Placeholder—allows a temporary name to be applied that can be filled in later.

Add New Source—opens a pop-up box for citation information to be filled in.

- Click on Show All Bibliography Fields to see all the fill-in box options.
- Add page numbers in document by clicking on the generated citation and clicking edit citation.

Once the information is added, click Insert Citation. A drop-down menu will appear housing the citations. Click the needed citation, and the information appears in the document.

At the end of the document, a list resembling the table of contents but for references can be generated the same way via the Bibliography drop-down menu.

Helpful Hint: Similar to importing styles from other documents, Word gives the same option to sources via the Manage Sources option.

Helpful Hints and Shortcuts

Writer Trick #2

Instead of highlighting by clicking inside the text, hover on the left-hand side of the page until your cursor changes into an arrow. Once it does, click and drag to highlight a single row of text or entire swaths of text without having to drag across the pages.

Writer Trick #3

Sometimes the Home bar and subsequent menus will disappear. If that happens, click on the upward-facing arrow to have them redisplayed.

Decorative Borders and Lines

Sometimes three asterisks, equal signs, or underscores will cause a "decorative" border to appear. If they are not wanted, there are three ways to remove/prevent them.

- Option 1—Immediately hit the undo (Ctrl+z) button or backspace and hit Return again. This is not the most efficient way.
- Option 2—Prevent it before it happens. File > Options > Proofing > AutoCorrect Options x2 (The section is labelled AutoCorrect Options and the button is also labeled AutoCorrect Options)> A new pop-up appears, choose the AutoCorrect As You Type tab > Uncheck the Border Lines option.

- Option 3A—Underneath the Pilcrow is a border option. Click "No Borders."
- Option 3B—There is a more detailed border option under the Design tab. Design tab > Page Borders > Borders and Shading pop-up appears > click None in the left hand column > On the right-hand side of the pop-up just above the OK and Cancel buttons is a drop-down menu to choose specific pages or the entire document to apply the effect to.

Code Shortcuts

The Alt, Ctrl, and Shift keys, when used with a set of letters and numbers, become a shortcut to many functions. Many of these codes will work on websites and social media.

Alt Codes

Alt codes create situations or symbols in text instead of having to open extra windows to select special characters. This is a short list, but a simple Google search of Alt Codes for Windows will give an entire list from letters of the alphabet to punctuation and more.

- Alt+0151: —
- Alt+0162: ¢ (cents)
- Alt+0153: ™ (trademark symbol)
- Alt+0169: © (copyright symbol)
- Alt+F7: find the next misspelling or grammatical error
- Alt+F8: run a macro

Ctrl Codes

Useful All-Purpose

- Ctrl+mouse wheel: zoom in and out.
- Ctrl+z: undoes the last move made.
- Ctrl+s: saves the document.
- Ctrl+a: selects all
- Ctrl+c: copies highlighted text
- Ctrl+v: pastes the copied information
- Ctrl+n: new document
- Ctrl+p: print
- Ctrl+Enter: page break
- Ctrl+F2: open print window

Justification

- Ctrl+j: changes the line to justified
- Ctrl+l: the line to Aligned Left
- Ctrl+e: centers selected text
- Ctrl+r: aligns text to the right
- Ctrl+k: opens the hyperlink pop-up where you can insert URLs.

Font Options

- Ctrl+d: opens the Font pop-up
- Ctrl+b: bolds text
- Ctrl+i: applies italics
- Ctrl+u: underline
- Ctrl+=: apply subscript $_{\text{formatting}}$
- Ctrl+spacebar: remove formatting on the character/word level
- Ctrl+q: remove paragraph formatting

- Ctrl+1: single space line spacing
- Ctrl+2: double space line spacing
- Ctrl+5: 1.5 line spacing

Moving Cursor

- Ctrl+End: moves cursor to the end of the line
- CRTL+Home: moves cursor to the beginning of the line

Shift Codes

Useful Codes

- Shift+F1: opens the reveal formatting tab. I haven't talked about this. It can show what styles have been applied without opening up different windows.
- Shift+F2: copy text
- Shift+F3: cycle through the case changes.
- Shift+F4: cycle through the words that fit the "find" feature.
- Shift+F5: takes you to the last place you were typing/editing
- Shift+F7: open the thesaurus
- Shift+F10: open the right click menu
- Shift+F12: save

Selecting Text

- Shift+right arrow: select a single character to the right (space, letter, etc)
- Shift+ left arrow: select a single character to the left
- Shift+End: select text to the end of the line
- Shift+Home: select text to the beginning of the line

- Shift+ down arrow or up arrow: select one line above or below

Ctrl+Shift Codes

Font Options

- Ctrl+Shift+F: Font Popup Window
- Ctrl+Shift+P: Font Popup Window
- Ctrl+Shift+>: increase font size
- Ctrl+Shift+<: decrease font size
- Ctrl+Shift+w: underline words but not spaces
- Ctrl+Shift+d: double-underline text
- Ctrl+Shift+k: SMALL LETTER CAPS
- Ctrl+Shift+(plus sign): apply superscript ^{formatting}
- Ctrl+Shift+m: remove a paragraph indent
- Ctrl+Shift+s: apply a style (it opens a small pop-up box)
- Ctrl+Shift+F9: remove hyperlink from selected text

Other Useful Codes

- Ctrl+Shift+enter: insert a column break
- Ctrl+Shift+spacebar: insert a non-breaking space

Selecting Text

- Ctrl+Shift+left or right arrow: select from wherever the cursor is to the end of the word in the direction you pick
- Ctrl+Shift+down arrow: select the text to the end of the paragraph (picking the up arrow will select it to the beginning of the paragraph)

- Ctrl+Page Up (or Down): selects the page of text above or below where your cursor is. This is not done by what you think of as a page. What I mean is if your cursor is at the top of the page, then it'll go to the bottom, but if your cursor is in the middle, it will go to the middle of the previous/next page.
- Ctrl+Shift+Home: select text to the beginning of the document
- Ctrl+Shift+End: select text to the end of the document

Alt+Ctrl Codes

Font Options

- Alt+Ctrl+1: apply Heading Style 1
- Alts+Ctrl+2: apply Heading Style 2
- Alt+Ctrl+3: apply Heading Style 3

Short Cut Codes

- Alt+Ctrl+c: ©
- Alt+Ctrl+r: ®
- Alt+Ctrl+t: ™
- Alt+Ctrl+. (period): …
- Alt+Ctrl+f: insert footnote
- Alt+Ctrl+e: insert endnote

DELETE Codes

- Backspace: deletes one character (single space, single letter)
- Ctrl+Backspace: delete one word to the left
- Ctrl+Delete: delete one word to the right

Macros

For writers with complex character names or magical spells that are cast repeatedly can save time with Macros. A Macro is a preprogramed action similar to speed dial. Once it is set up, activating the macro causes the action to repeat, much like speed dial has phone numbers programmed.

On the View tab near the end is a Macro drop-down. It comes with 2 options:

- View Macros
- Record Macro

To make a Macro, click on Record Macro. Name it something logical and decide if it becomes a button on the ribbon bar or assigned to a keyboard.

- Option 1: Button (Ribbon Binding)

  Clicking the Button option will open the Word Options box. It will appear in the left-hand column (1). By clicking Add (2), the Macro will shift to the right-hand column (3) and appear on the bar. Dragging it up and down in the right-hand column to adjust where on the bar it appears. Then click Save (4). (Jump to Macro Recording).

- Option 2: Keyboard (Key Binding)

  Clicking on the Keyboard Option will bring up another pop-up box. Assign the keyboard sequence to trigger it in the "Press new shortcut key."

Macro Recording

Recording the Macro is the same for either placement option. Follow the prompts on the screen to start and stop the recording. The Macro drop-down box will allow an action to be paused or stopped. Stopping the Macro locks in what was recorded.

Captions and Cross-reference

Captions

Some books come with tons of images and graphics. These images can be labeled, and a table of figures can be created sequentially to help readers navigate to specific sections.

First, the images need to be labeled. On the Reference tab, click Insert Caption. The Caption pop-up box will appear. Name the picture, label what type it is and assign a location for this information to appear.

To create a table of figures, place the cursor where the table is to go, and click Insert Table of Figures. It works the same way a table of contents does by looking for the information supplied by the labeled images.

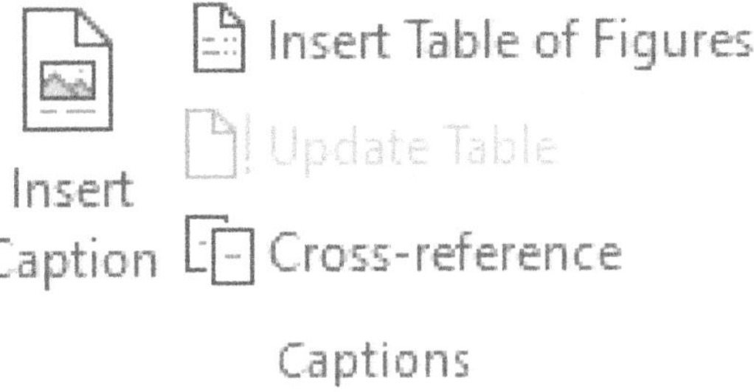

Cross-reference

Occasionally, sections will reference another area of the document. An example of this might be in a cookbook when referencing an icing recipe given pages earlier or later in the book or a map in the front or back matter of the book.

Click the cross-reference at the bottom of the Captions section of the Reference tab. The Cross-reference pop-up box will appear. The drop-down menu will generate a short list of items that can be cross-linked to (based on images and graphic captions). Similar to the footnote/endnotes, click where the link needs to appear, and click Insert. The names become hyperlinks, and when clicked moves the reader to the appropriate table/graph if they are reading it on their computer or phone.

Indexes

In the back of textbooks and recipe books are pages of key words and their page numbers, normally labeled as an index, and if you've ever thought about how that was created, it was done through Indexes, which is similar to cross-reference. Word has a built-in option to help generate these types of list.

Highlight the word that needs to be indexed, and click Mark Entry. The Mark Entry pop-up box will appear. Main entry will be the word highlighted, and if a subcategory needs to be created, it can be added in the Subentry box. Under Options, the program can search and mark words within a page range or limited to just the page where the mark entry is used. Bold and italic check boxes affect the index appearance when it is generated.

There are two options:

- Mark—only the word highlighted is targeted.
- Mark All—All references for the word within the page ranges will be referenced.

Once finished, the pop-up box will disappear, and the word(s) referenced will have a unique tag following each word.

To generate the Index, put the cursor where the list needs to start and hit "Insert Index."

Tab Stops

Tabs are frowned upon in submissions and publications, but sometimes they can serve a purpose, like keeping the word count from spilling across two lines on a short-story submission.

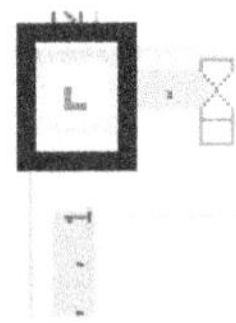

There is a little box at the top of the ruler that has seven symbols, and each is responsible for something different. Hover the cursor over the symbol to read the different options, and click the box to cycle through the options. The two most important ones are the forward and backward L tab stops.

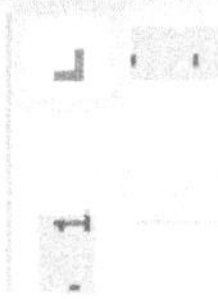

The standard L keeps all the text to the left of its placement, keeping the tab space the same distance. This is what most people are familiar with.

The backward L prevents the text from going past the marker, and the tab space shrinks to accommodate the additional words.

Change the box to the needed symbol, and click on the ruler. It will appear on the ruler. To adjust its location, slide it along the ruler, or drag down to remove it.

Embedding Fonts and Saving as PDF

Word does not automatically embed fonts. Embedded fonts lets anyone open the file and see it exactly the way intended. To embed, click Options > Save > Preserve Fidelity when sharing this document > click Embed Fonts in File and uncheck the two sub-boxes.

This is important if the PDF generated is being used at companies like Kindle Direct Publishing or IngramSpark.

To save as a PDF, click File > Save As > PDF.

**If images are not appearing in the PDF correctly, make sure the images are JPEG.

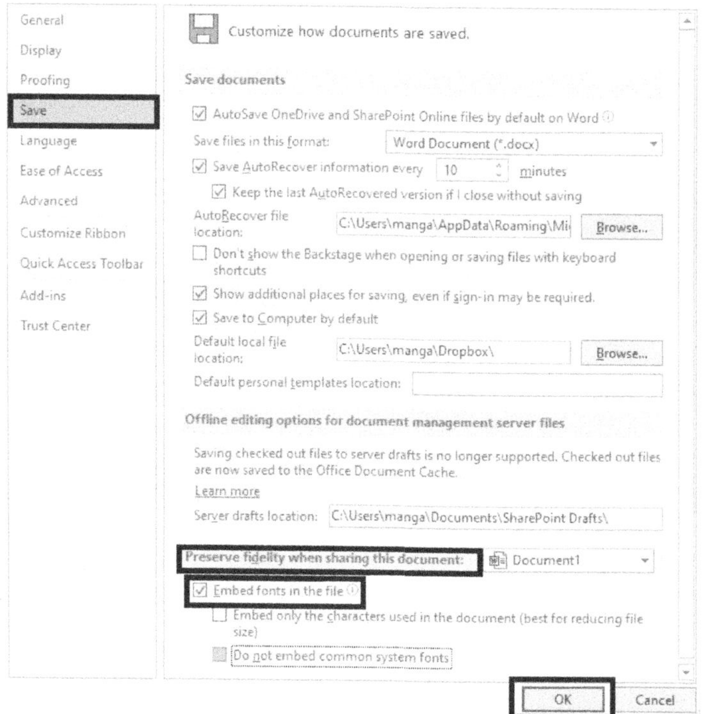

Part 2: Submission Formatting

Whether someone knows the name or not, Shunn format is the standard for submissions. It has been around since the late eighties and was created by William Shunn who had firsthand knowledge and experience in the field of publishing. On his website, www.shunn.net, he has guides for short stories, novels, and poems.

This section will cover how the submission layout for short stories and novels are laid out. Please check submission guidelines before submitting. They may want different formatting than Shunn, but, with the parts covered in part one, you can save time adjusting the file to fit the requirements.

Short Stories

From micro-fiction to short stories, these quick reads have gained in popularity. Programs like Duotrope and Submission Grinder make submissions easy to find and track.

Setting up the document:

Short Story Submission Checklist:

- 1" margins (Word's default setting)
- Standard page size 8.5" by 11" (Word's default setting)
- 12pt font in Times New Roman or Courier
- Address top left-hand corner single spaced
- Word count on the same line as name
- Title 1/3 of the way down the page
- Story immediately follows and is double spaced with .5" indented paragraphs

The upper corner is the author info. This contains the writer's real name (legal name for tax/payment issues), word count, address, email, and relevant organizations. This information is single spaced. Please don't omit address or email. If the submission editor has questions or needs to get ahold of you, phone and email are the two best ways. If a magazine does contributor copies, they need a way to mail you the copy instead of spending days waiting for a response to an email.

Word count is the story not the address section, title, or byline. There are two ways to find word count: bottom of the document on the left-hand side or on the Review tab. If any text is selected, then the word count will reflect the highlighted text and not the entire document.

Round the word count to the nearest hundred, or, if the fiction piece is flash fiction or smaller, round to the nearest fifty. Example: 3,564 words is 3,600. 3,235 words is 3,200. Publishers use these numbers to determine how much room a story will take up.

The word count is put on the same row as the real name, and to get it across the page without a million spaces requires a tab stop.

Find the right tab stop (backward L) and click on the ruler to place it between the last two dashes of the right indent marker (the triangle looking shape marking the margin). If it is misplaced, it can be slid left or right along the ruler or pulled down to remove completely.

Once the tab is placed, place the cursor at the end of the name and hit tab. The space will between name and word count will shrink or grow while leaving the word count flush against the margin.

The title and byline (pen name/publishing name) are centered and roughly a third of the way down the page. Use the Paragraph Spacing Before option to move the title down the page instead of multiple returns.

This blank space is where publishers/agents staple the pages and make notes for themselves and others.

Skip a line. The story goes after the title and byline and is double spaced.

At the end of the story, drop down one line and, centered, type The End or End. This signals to the agent or submission editor that no pages were omitted or misplaced.

On page two, click on the header. Check mark "Different First Page" and no check mark in "Different Even and Odd."

Right align the text and type the writer's last name/keywords of the title/page number.

Example: Rowling / Harry Potter Sorcerer's Stone / 2

If the writer's last name is common (Jones, Smith, etc.), please feel free to add the first initial followed by a period to the header.

Example: J. Rowling / Harry Potter Sorcerer's Stone / 2

This information is right aligned, because it could be printed out and stapled, obscuring the information.

Congratulations. You've formatted your short story

See the following page for a visual of the short story layout. It is not to scale due to book size.

Legal Name
Street Address
County, State, Zip
Phone Number
Email

about 1,500 words

Relevant Groups

Story Title

by Publishing Name

The story starts here and is double spaced. The rest will be in generated text to give you a visual reference.

Quissun tureped molor sitiam audametur, ullitatus esto officae quis doles iscium re soluptam soloria vendunti dolest que nonse occuptia iur?

Um quo te lam, int. Em que ipisimus eos aliat omnihitio doluptat.

Lorem ipsum dolor sit amet, consectetur adipiscing elit, sed do eiusmod tempor incididunt ut labore et dolore magna aliqua. Molestie ac feugiat sed lectus vestibulum mattis ullamcorper velit. Felis eget nunc lobortis mattis.

Eget felis eget nunc lobortis mattis aliquam faucibus purus. Ullamcorper a lacus vestibulum sed arcu non odio. Non diam phasellus vestibulum lorem.

Fermentum posuere urna nec tincidunt praesent semper feugiat nibh sed. Sed risus pretium quam vulputate dignissim suspendisse in est ante. Eu non diam phasellus vestibulum lorem sed risus ultricies tristique. Risus nullam eget felis eget nunc lobortis mattis. Augue ut lectus arcu bibendum at varius vel pharetra.

A pellentesque sit amet porttitor eget dolor. Neque gravida in fermentum et sollicitudin ac. Turpis egestas sed tempus urna et pharetra pharetra massa massa. Ut ornare lectus sit amet est placerat. Rhoncus est pellentesque elit ullamcorper dignissim cras tincidunt. Vitae et leo duis ut diam quam nulla porttitor massa. Mi tempus imperdiet nulla malesuada pellentesque

End

Novels

The only notable difference between short-story submissions and novel submissions is the first page and how to handle chapters. Again, I must stress, read all the submission guidelines before submitting. If they don't specify, submitting Shunn is the most likely choice.

Novel Submission Checklist:

- 1" margins (Word's default setting)
- Standard page size 8.5" by 11" (Word's default setting)
- Address top left-hand corner single spaced
- 12pt font in Times New Roman or Courier
- Title and byline a 1/3 of the way down the page
- Word count at the bottom of first page
- Story starts on the second page and is double spaced with .5" indented paragraphs

The same address information used in short-story format is applied to longer-length word submissions. It all goes in the top left-hand corner except word count.

Midway down the page, the title and byline are centered. The word count is rounded to the nearest hundred and is centered at the bottom of the page.

For both title/byline and word count, use the Paragraph Spacing Before option to move them down the page instead of multiple returns.

Similar to short stories, set up the header to have a different first page and the same even/odd pages.

The same information is applied: initial period space last name / keywords of your title / page number

The chapter begins a third of the way down the page. Skip two lines between chapter name and the story body, which is double spaced. This is done for all chapters. To move chapters to the next page, apply a page break at the end of the chapter. This will continue through all requested pages or full manuscript request.

If it's a full manuscript request, end the story with The End/ End centered, but, if it's a partial, then do not.

**If the time was taken to create styles, moving the start of chapters is a two second click instead of multiple returns or multiple mouse clicks in the before Paragraph Spacing Option.

Legal Name
Street Address
County, State, Zip
Phone Number
Email

Relevant Groups

Story Title

by Publishing Name

about 60,000 words

Chapter 1

Chapter Names (Optional)

Remember chapters always start on their own page, and are a third of the way down the page. Similar to short stories, the paragraphs are indented and double spaced.

Vendunti dolest que nonse occuptia iur?

Um quo te lam, int. Em que ipisimus eos aliat omnihitio doluptat.

Lorem ipsum dolor sit amet, consectetur adipiscing elit, sed do eiusmod tempor incididunt ut labore et dolore magna aliqua. Molestie ac feugiat sed lectus vestibulum mattis ullamcorper velit. Felis eget nunc lobortis mattis.

Submission Letters

Cover letters and query letters, not to be confused with synopsis, overlap in some details, such as containing key information about the story, but cover letters tend to be used with short stories and query letters are novel oriented.

THE LETTER SHOULD NOT EXCEED ONE PAGE. I'll repeat that: It should not exceed one page. Yes, we all like to think our work is an exception, but this is one rule that has no allowances.

Query and cover letters should include relevant facts, and these facts should strengthen why the writer is an authority on the topic.

If the story is about a teenage witch learning to grow a garden with her powers and the writer is a member of the local chapter of XYZ plants or the Lily Club, that is relevant. If the same book is written by someone who has never gardened and the only accolades they could sprout is being in the Mile High Club, then it shouldn't be included as relevant information.

Keep the paragraphs short. Put a space between the paragraphs to prevent it becoming a wall of text. Along with increasing readability, it also shows the writer can highlight relevant information and not go overboard on the details.

Cover Letter (Short Story)

You can have written the most iconic, the best piece of fiction ever created, but if you can't write a decent cover letter, the chances of having it read are rather slim. These letters help a submission editor weed through the submissions without having to spend time reading a story and wasting time.

The cover letter is the first thing a submission editor will see, and it goes with a completed short-story submission. It serves the following purposes:

- If the story is a good fit.
- Personal experience to give the story credit.
- Can the writer write?
- If it is a blind submission (your submission is submitted with your name and any identifying markers removed), they can match writer to submission after they make their decisions.
- Sometimes papers just get separated

Cover letters are usually sent by email with your submission attached. Occasionally, you'll paste the body of your submission in the email if it's under a certain word count. If this happens, do your cover letter first, then, under your email signature, paste the story.

Keys to Cover Letters

- Make it personal, but don't confuse that with intimate.
- Address the submission editor or editors directly.
- If you can't find their names, addressing it to the Submission Editor or Editor will be okay.
- If you didn't take the time to even look and the editor's name is easy to find, it will affect the perception of you.

The first paragraph is not a sales pitch.

- It is about the story: title, word count, genre.
- If you are submitting it to a specific contest or anthology, mention so. A publisher may have multiple open submissions.

The second paragraph, if needed, gives credit to your story.

- If you're writing about the American Revolution and you are a historian or reenactor, it would be worth mentioning. If it's just a short story and you don't have anything that would support the work, don't bother filling this section in with fluff. Maybe talk about your other publications, or just skip it entirely.

The third paragraph, thank the editor and the publication by name.

End it with your name, your email address, and your phone number. Don't crowd your signature. It looks sloppy.

Pretty boring, right? A submission editor doesn't need the writer's life story. The work should speak for itself. They may have one a day come across their desk or have hundreds.

Query Letters (Full Manuscripts)

Query letters may be the hardest thing an author will write. It should be short but contain enough of the sense of the story and your writing style to catch the attention of an editor. Since so much of fiction is a matter of taste, the letter needs to be targeted to the publisher as much as possible.

Read the submission guidelines carefully. Some agents or publishers will detail exactly how they want the letter drafted, down to the order of information provided. For others not as fully detailed, you'll follow the general cover letter with a few minor differences.

- If you met the agent/publisher before or received an offer to submit through #PitMad, mention it before getting into the heart of things. If you have no connection to the agent/publisher, jump straight into the story.
- Similar to cover letters, mention the book by name, give the genre, word count, and if it is a completed manuscript.
- Now hook the agent/publisher into reading your work. You'll have 5-7 sentences, and I wouldn't recommend pushing past that. Don't worry if it contains spoilers. This isn't the blurb, but do try to cover your main character, the main plot, and conflict.
- If you can add anything that gives your book credit, then do so, but don't list things irrelevant to the story or your career as a writer.

Example:

Submission Editor,

I met you at the Tennessee Writers Conference in Knoxville in July. I'm following up with *Free Flowing Liquids.* You praised it for being a unique reflection of the 1920s and the underlying problems veterans faced.

Jim B, a bootlegger, is trying to survive after returning home from World War 1. The stores and the town may not have changed, but home wasn't what it was. For Jim, carving a living on either side of the law meant providing for what was left of his family. Trying to do the best he can just became more dangerous with a decision that could put the life of his little sister in the crosshairs.

Free Flowing Liquids is a completed 80,000-word historical novel set in the era of the US prohibition. This is my fifth novel set in the rural south.

Thank you and your staff. I look forward to hearing from you.

Kari Holloway
Email
(###)-###-####

The example letter references the fact that I met the submission editor at a conference, brings to the front what he said about it, then it goes into the story like any other agent/publisher would get. Just because you remember the agent/publisher doesn't mean they remember you.

Is it a perfect example? No. There isn't any such thing as a perfect letter. But there are plenty of examples of bad ones.

The people reading these are human and their tastes vary. What works for one might not work with another. If you write a convincing query, an agent/publisher may request a synopsis or tell you to send part or whole manuscript.

Query Letters (Nonfiction)

For nonfiction, there are two types of queries: Narrative Driven and Information Driven.

- Narrative Driven: biographies, memoirs, etc.
- Information Driven: "How to" guides

These are pitched usually before writing them, but don't let that hold you back.

Laid out like novel query letters, the only main difference is the addition of market. You'll want to detail who would be interested in the book and what your book provides.

- What you're selling: genre/category, anticipated word count, title/subtitle
- What makes your book unique or its unique selling proposition
- Target readership: who will buy this book and why? (it cannot be everyone and anyone)
- Your bio, platform, and credentials to write the book
- Thank you and closing

Synopsis

Synopsis comes after the query or sometimes accompanies a query. Read the agent/publisher's website before sending unwarranted information.

The synopsis seems foreboding. It is supposed to detail your story, but it shouldn't be this monstrous long process either.

Here are my helpful hints

- It's okay to put spoilers. This isn't the blurb.
- The agent/publisher wants to make sure the story progresses well before reading 40,000 words plus.
- Written in the present tense.
- Keep the emotion out of it.
- If your synopsis does its job, the agent/publisher will get the emotion from the manuscript.

If you outline, your synopsis will be easier to write, since you'll already have notes documenting the progression of the story. For pantsers, the task may take a little more effort.

Take a key point from each chapter, and use other sentences to weave them together. It's that simple.

Here is the actual synopsis I used for my first book, *Cracked but Never Broken*. I received 5 full manuscript requests.

> Damien Payne returns home to the Laughing P. His intentions are to settle down and take up the mantle of running the family's ranch. The same day home, he manages to insult the love of his life, discover he has a niece and nephew, and Maw-Payne whacks him with a spoon. If that's not enough, now he must go apologize to the quiet girl next door—Lexi.
>
> After he convinces Lexi to let him in the door, he apologizes and sees pictures of the life he's missed while overseas. Curiosity peaks as he discovers a scar on Lexi, but unwilling to get into another fight, he's

content to just hold the woman he loves for the night.

Early morning dawns, and Maw-Payne brings the unwelcomed news—rustlers have cut through the fence. A stalker leaves a surprise for all. With a job to do, Lexi promises she'll explain what is going on when she can. Someone needs to; Damien feels lost in a world he grew up in.

Pizza and booze make for a great afternoon with a friend, but John has another motive. Ralph, John's brother, is blackmailing him. John has no choice but to knock out his friend.

Damien awakes chained to the heavy chair in the bedroom of his home. Ralph wastes no time setting the mood. Candles burn, and Ralph's favorite toys are laid out. Unbeknown to Lexi, she's walking into a trap.

What feels like an eternity, Ralph enjoys using the cattle prod after he shows Damien his handiwork on Lexi's back. Ralph's greed for revenge is his downfall as Lexi kills him. Damien overcomes with the grief that he couldn't save her himself turns to booze to quiet his demons.

If life couldn't get more complicated, Donna—his on-again/off-again lover—is

> the puppeteer of Ralph. It comes to light that Donna is more than an innocent bystander. She goes to extremes to drive Damien back into her arms.
>
> Damien thought life should continue just as it was. He had a plan. Yet, his actions have left his relationship with Lexi broken. In the spur of the moment scramble, he proposes, and she can't accept. She tries to tell him she loves him but isn't in love with him. In a fit of rage, he grabs her. He's afraid of letting her go, but one thing Lexi doesn't abide is the physical beginnings of abuse, even accidental abuse.
>
> Darien, his twin brother, takes him outside to the barn. Fixing the barn seems pointless when all Damien wants is to solve his problems with Lexi. As he watches Darien and Lexi talk, he comes to the stark reality that his brother is in love with Lexi.
>
> Unable to fix what he broke, unable to bear the pain seeped into his home, unable to face the talk of a small-town, Damien sets his home on fire. The first that rages inside is the turmoil that ebbs and flows within him.

It reads like a textbook or a history channel narrative. It should. The point of the synopsis is for the submission editor or agent to follow the progression of the story. Does it have enough conflict? Does it make sense? Does it follow the norm of the genre? These single-page writeups answer so many questions, and if it fits all the boxes for the publication/agent, then you did your job well.

Follow Up

Realize that submission editors are people, and they have a complicated job. Turnaround time might be a few days, or they could take six months or longer. Don't harass them with follow-up requests unless they have had it longer than their website states. Send them a simple "I was inquiring if you had received my letter about *Book Title*." If you don't hear back, strike them from your list, and move on.

When you get a rejection letter, don't reply defending your book. It is unprofessional. Take their advice and apply it or ignore it. If you can't say anything nice, don't say anything at all. Generally, I send back a "Thank you for your time and advice. Have a great day (or Happy Holidays, if it's around the holidays)," sign it with my name and email address/website and move on. Many times, the "thank you" garners no further response from the publication, but sometimes I've gotten a heads up on either imprint presses looking for something similar to what I submitted or what contests will be announced soon.

No matter which one you'll need, if you plan on having any traditional publications, one or all will become an intimate part of your wheelhouse. Take a breath, make a list of key points that you need to cover and try to not be the doting parent to your work.

Publishers vs Vanity

The most common thing I hear in writer's groups is "I paid my publisher $5k …" Let's not finish that sentence. It already contains a huge red flag. In this part, I'll give you a quick guide to traditional publishing, vanity publishing, and self-publishing.

Traditional Publishing

Traditional publishers can be huge corporations or small one/two person operations. It's not the size of the office staff that makes it a traditional publisher.

They read your manuscript, and if they like it, they offer you a contract. If you're like Stephen King, you'll get an advance, but, for most authors, don't expect one. They take your manuscript and handle the cost of everything from editing to proofing, cover designs, audio, and have a modest marketing budget.

You never pay to be published by a traditional publisher. Sometimes you might need an agent to submit a manuscript to a top-tier publisher, but hundreds take unsolicited manuscripts.

Agents

The point of an agent is to represent your manuscripts to publishers that are a good fit. This could include audio, foreign, film, as well as the book. Agents understand contracts, and they negotiate contract terms and can often act as go-betweens for author/publisher issues that arise.

You do not pay agents; they get paid a percentage of the royalties—there is a standard amount across the board. In the US, a literary agent's commission is 15% of royalties, or 20-25% for foreign or subsidiary. They do not charge for reading or submitting your work; they make money when you make money.

If you're looking for someone to get you into book readings, festivals, and such, you want a publicist not an agent.

Vanity Publishing

They look like a traditional publisher. They have the fancy sites; they say they'll handle everything from editing to audio and beyond. Sounds good except:

- They offer you a contract before even reading your work.
- They want money to publish.
- They tend to harass you with phone calls and emails.

Everything is available for an "extra" fee that puts the prices higher than top-tier market prices. Either way, run. If you're going to pay, go self-published.

Hybrid Publishing

This term has been around a few decades, and they walk a fine line with vanity publishing. These have the nice websites, they offer author services, and the author has creative control.

A good hybrid publisher, unlike vanity, doesn't accept everything that gets submitted. They tend to offer a better royalty rate than a traditional publisher, and some of their after-publication services may come with a price tag or a longer contract to recoup the cost in royalties.

My two cents: hybrid may take a lot of the marketing and nit-picky stuff, but, if you're not writing series and can turn out multiple books a year, you might be better off perfecting your query letter for traditional publishing or saving up and self-publishing. Numbers-crunch wise, you won't make enough off a single book to make their services worthwhile.

Indie

Indie gets thrown around, and in the last couple of years, a shift has occurred in the meaning of the word.

In the fashion of indie-music labels, indie can mean an independent label who provides traditional publishing services but on a smaller scale. Some of these are hybrid publishing companies, while others are traditional.

Most self-publishers use the term because they are independent. They can adhere to traditional lines of writing what sells, or they can tackle the market and forge a new path. They can make the market bend to them if their writing is good enough. They are not reined in except by their own limits … they are indie.

Self-publishing

You're the publisher. You handle finding people to edit, format, design the covers, narrate, and every expense imaginable. Your budget is what you can handle. Your promos are what you find. You handle everything unless you can afford a personal assistant.

The only people you pay are people you contract to do so. Most of these will be freelancers, and some of the print-on-demand (POD) services offer these services as well (and they tend to be higher than average market rates), and the spectrum of cost will vary between them due to experience, time investment, specifics of the job, deadline, and how sought after the freelancer is.

DEGREES DO NOT NECESSARILY MEAN THEY ARE GOOD AT THE JOB

Always vet before you hire. Look at their portfolio, ask other writers to see if they have used them, check out the sample of the work they should provide for you, talk to them. Talk to them? Yes. A good freelancer should understand the market. If you're writing historical fiction, you need someone who understands that some words and phrases didn't exist, that languages have evolved greatly since then, and they shouldn't be trying to modernize things if they understand the genre. If you're writing science fiction, you'll want someone who understands the genre. Cover designers should know what current trends are moving toward or what designs are falling out of favor. Look at their portfolio and see if they make covers similar to the top 50 in your genre. If they do, you probably want to contact them.

A good freelancer will give you reasons why they recommend things and be willing to answer questions. They might have a degree, or they might have just been born with the knack or gained their talent through experience, but regardless of how they came to be a freelancer, vet their current work.

Compare the numbers

The average eBook is $2.99 on Amazon. Amazon gives you a 70% cut after they take their delivery fee.

We'll say you make $2.09 after Amazon does their thing.

With traditional, you would probably get 20-30%= $0.62, but you didn't have to find or pay for anything to get the book to that point.

Vanity, you're already $5k in the hole. With the books generally well out of normal price ranges and the lack of actual editing and such, you might never recover the money you already invested.

Hybrid, we'll go with a 50/50 split. That makes your payment $1.04. Depending on the services you use, you may or may not recoup the money, but that lays largely on the marketing the hybrid publisher provides.

With self-publishing, you may have spent $1,000, probably less, to cover editing, covers, and even some marketing. You'll make the full $2.09, and by following market advice in such groups as 20booksto50k, you'll recoup that within 5 years for the average writer, while some recoup it in considerably less time.

Part 3: Publication Formatting

Formatting for publication can be broken down by standard and genre explicit.

The differences boil down to two things: indents and font choices.

Indents

For nonfiction, none of the paragraphs are indented, and there is a small space between paragraphs. The spacing between paragraphs are up to the writer, but standard would be 6pt or 8pt. That said, there are plenty of examples out there that apply fiction formatting. So do research on the specific style of nonfiction you're writing, and go with what a majority of current works are doing.

In fiction, the first paragraphs at the beginning of the chapter, after a scene break, and after a soft scene break are not indented, while the paragraphs that follow are indented. These starter paragraphs are not indented because, what if that paragraph starts at the top of a page? It is a clear indication of a shift in the scene.

Fonts

Many fonts come standard in Microsoft Word, and through sites like Fontbundles.net, writers can download commercial approved fonts. Do not take fonts and use them in print and eBook if the license for the font is not commercial. That is theft.

Some fonts, like Caslon, are used mainly in nonfiction. These fonts have a long history and have been around since the invention of the printing press and are good fonts to begin with. Other fonts are rather new; Calibri was invented in 2007, and that actually helped with a court case where fraud was determined due to the age of the font.

The key to choosing fonts are:

Limit a book to 2-4 fonts. This can be a font for title pages, one for chapter headings, and one for the story. If the font is hard to read, readers won't finish it. To see if a font pair looks good or is readable, print a page of the story in the chosen fonts, and fold it in your lap, and read it. If the words become jumbled, either replace the font choice, or increase the line spacing.

Popular Font Options for Fiction

- Garamond
- Minion Pro
- Palatino

Layout

Books have a standard layout that is more of a guideline. The invention of the eBook and the explosion of indie writers have led to a nonstandard approach. The only thing that has stayed consistent is the inclusion of a title page before the story. The following section covers what the parts are and the basic layout. Not every book needs every section, and the sections included can be rearranged.

Book half-title

- Contains the title of the book.

Title page

- Contains title and author byline.

- Does not need the word By Author Name unless this is a book full of illustrations or images and both author and illustrator are fighting for cover space.

Copyright page

- This can be as simple as Copyright © Year Name.
- The ISBN is found on this page.
- This page should contain contact information in case someone wants to get ahold of the writer or publisher.

Also by

- While not important in the front matter as much as it does in the back matter, a handy checklist can lead readers to more works by you or a clear indication they are reading books out of order.

Dedication

- Do not confuse this with an acknowledgment.
- This is where a writer can do an "in honor of" type thing.

Acknowledgments

- This is the place to thank all the people who helped make your book what it is.

Table of Contents

- This is needed in eBooks.
- The only time a paperback needs a TOC:

Anthology with multiple writers and stories.
A collection containing many stories.
A boxset that contains multiple books.
Most nonfiction

Foreword

- A forward and preface get confused often. A foreword is written by someone other than the author and is always signed by the crafter of it. Generally, it tells of an interaction between them and the author and a little bit about the story the reader is about to read.

Preface

- A preface is generally written by the author and details how a book came about. Less common in fiction, it may accompany books with deep roots to real events, and it details the credits of the author. If it's a crime drama, a background in criminology or even being a reformed criminal would lend credibility to the work.

Introduction

- This is written by the author and tells how the story came to be.

Epigraph

- This is a quote that contains meaning to the author and maybe in relation to the book.
- This generally goes right before the story or under a chapter heading.

Call-to-action (CTA)

- This is anything that is trying to get the reader to do something. This can be joining a newsletter, following on social media, or leaving a review.

About the Author

- This one is entirely subjective.

Is this all? No. The list is extensive, but these are the most common things.

Styles

Styles will make formatting easier. The most basic styles to start with are:

- Title
- 2nd Title
- Author Name
- Copyright
- Heading style 1 which will be used as chapter titles
- 1st paragraphs (not indented)
- 2nd paragraphs (indented unless it's nonfiction)
- Scene Breaks

Depending on the story, more styles may need to be added.

Trim Size

The trim size refers to the size of the book, and the options are numerous. The print-on-demand service used will have an available list.

The most common sizes are:

- 5” by 8”
- 5.25” by 8”
- 5.5” by 8.5”
- 6” by 9”

The two things that determine trim size are word count and reader expectation.

The larger the word count, the bigger the book. A 6” by 9” easily holds 120,000 words but would look rather thin with a 40,000-word story. The opposite is true to a 5” by 8” would make a 50,000-word story look like a decent length read, and a 120,000-word story would look like a dictionary and be uncomfortable to read.

Stay consistent with series.

To set the trim size, go to Layout > Size, and input the trim size and margins > Apply to entire document.

Page Numbering

Once the trim has been applied, the only thing left is to apply the author's name, book title, and page number to the header header/footer.

Go to the page prior to Chapter 1, and insert a section break. On the first page of chapter 1, unlink the header/footer from the previous section. Set that page to be page one under format page numbers on the header/footer bar. Unlink the header/footer for the next two pages.

Unlinking the header/footers will preserve the empty header/footer of the front matter. The front matter doesn't need page numbers unless it is the roman numeral pages generally found in nonfiction.

The chapter starting position, author name, book title, and page number layouts vary between publishers and countries. Below is a general guideline, but check other books to determine how you want them to look.

Chapter Starting Positions

- Fall where they may—this means that when a section break is applied at the end of a chapter, the next chapter starts on the next page regardless if that page is an even/odd page.
- Always start on the odd page/right-hand side. When a section break is applied, an additional page break may be used to help shift the next chapter to fall on the next odd page. Hardback books are set this way.

Page numbers can go in 1 of 3 different locations:

- Outer top
- Bottom middle
- Outer bottom

Pages that chapters start on:

Header: blank

Footer

- Blank
- Page number centered

Option A:

Even page

- Header: author name and page number
- Footer: blank

Odd page

- Header: title and page number
- Footer: blank

Option B

Even page

- Header: title and page number
- Footer: blank

Odd page

- Header: chapter title and page number
- Footer: blank

Option C

Even page

- Header: author name and page number
- Footer: blank

Odd page

- Header: short-story name
- Footer: blank

Option D

Even page

- Header: book title and page number
- Footer: blank

Odd page

- Header: series title
- Footer: blank

Are these all the options? No. Just pick a style, and stay consistent. The information in the header/footer can be decorated using small caps, images, and such.

Sometimes the header/footer looks closer to the story than necessary. To help with visual appeal, apply 6pt or 8pt line spacing beneath the header and before the footer. Highlight the appropriate section, and apply. I consider this the safer approach.

eBooks

eBooks follow the same set up as print books minus the need for headers/footers and empty pages. While most retailers will take a Word document and auto convert it, I do not recommend doing this. Auto converters are to formatting as Grammarly is to an editor.

Auto converters cost you money in the long run with delivery fees because they add unnecessary code to the files. They also don't catch when something is formatted wrong.

For future information, upload ePub when able. It is a better formatted file. ePubs are also easier to edit in programs like Sigil than Mobis are. The difference is an ePub is built like books on a shelf—easily seen and easy to rearrange. Mobi files are built like a cake. Once it is baked, there isn't a good way to get the egg back out of it.

If you are intent on learning to format eBooks, I suggest using Calibre to convert a Word document to ePub and use Sigil for editing the eBooks. Sites like w3schools.com or YouTube can teach the basics of code.

That said, if Word is all you can work with, being able to apply styles will cut down on the number of auto converter glitches.

How to Handle Copyright & Plagiarism Infringement

All the labor of love and copyright notices won't stop thieves. It happens. With sites like Blasty, it has gotten easier to tackle the sites that pop-up, claiming they have your book for free. Most of the time, they are just phishing sites and don't even have your book.

Here is a list of websites to help you tackle the problem when you run across it. Remember rule number 1: don't comment, rant, rave, or drive any attention to them. It is a waste of your energy.

- kindlepreneur.com/ebook-piracy/
- helensedwick.com/step-by-step-guide-to-dealing-with-content-theft/
- www.plagiarismtoday.com/stock-letters/
- www.google.com/webmasters/tools/dmca-dashboard
- www.google.com/alerts#

Closing

Whether you're an aspiring writer, traditionally published, or self-published, understanding your tools will make your job easier.

I hope the information that preceded will help you now and in the future regardless of the path you choose.

While this is not everything you can do in Microsoft Word, it gives you enough to help get you started and give guidance as you find your feet and explore a new facet of yourself and the world you've entered.

The great thing about being human, regardless of our choices today, we can make different ones tomorrow. And the only failure in life is when we no longer try.

I hope your aspirations bring you good fortune and your pen never runs out of ink.

~Kari

***

For more information on publishing, check out writingwithoutdrama.com or follow on Facebook and Instagram.

Made in the USA
Coppell, TX
30 October 2021